W9-DFB-896

Chuck Yeager: The Man Who Broke the Sound Barrier

Chuck Yeager: The Man Who Broke the Sound Barrier

A Science Biography

by

Nancy Smiler Levinson

Walker and Company
New York

First published in the United States of America in 1988 by the Walker Publishing Company, Inc.

Published simultaneously in Canada by Thomas Allen & Son Canada, Limited, Markham, Ontario.

Library of Congress Cataloging-in-Publication Data

Levinson, Nancy Smiler
Chuck Yeager: the man who broke the sound barrier.

Bibliography: p.
Includes index.
Summary: A biography of the Air Force test pilot who in 1947 was the first man to fly faster than the speed of sound.
1. Yeager, Chuck, 1923– —Juvenile literature.
2. Air pilots—United States—Biography—Juvenile literature. [1. Yeager, Chuck, 1923– . 2. Air pilots]
I. Title.
TL540.Y4L48 1988 629.13'092'4 [B] [92] 87-25431
ISBN 0-8027-6781-8
ISBN 1-8027-6799-0 (reinf.)

Printed in the United States of America

2 4 6 8 10 9 7 5 3 1

Book design by Laurie McBarnette

For Ruth Cohen

ACKNOWLEDGMENTS

For assistance and continual good will during the preparation of this book, the author is deeply indebted to the Department of the United States Air Force, Headquarters Air Force Flight Test Center at Edwards AF Base, the base historians, and especially to TSgt. Lora J.S. Wray, NCOIC, of the Public Affairs Department.

Many others deserve acknowledgment as well: Joseph W. Hunnicutt III and the Society of Yeager Scholars of Marshall University, Gregory King, Maria T. Oharenko of the Northrop Corporation, Melissa Keiser of the National Air and Space Museum, Smithsonian Institution, Richard Burns, Linda Burns, Hettie Rousch, Hal Yeager Jr., Jake Marcum, Virginia Smith, Homer Hager Jr., Paul Bowles, Tim Massey, Don Marsh, Anita Mintz, Dr. Irwin A. Levinson, and Colonel Nate "Rube" Goldberg, U.S.A.F. (Ret.).

Important printed sources used were *Yeager* by Charles Yeager and Leo Janos, *Across the High Frontier: The Story of a Test Pilot* by William Lundgren, *Plane*

Talk edited by Carl R. Oliver, *They Flew Alone* by George Sullivan, *The Right Stuff* by Tom Wolfe, *Men in Space* by Shirley Thomas, and *The Lonely Sky* by Bill Bridgeman and Jacqueline Hazard. Other sources were *Current Biography*, *Colliers Magazine*, *Time*, *Newsweek*, *This Week*, *New York Times*, *Saturday Evening Post*, *Modern Maturity*, and *People*, and clippings from *Stars and Stripes* and the West Virginia newspapers the *Hamlin Lincoln Journal*, the *Huntington Advertiser*, the *Huntington Herald Dispatch*, and the *Charleston Gazette*.

The historians and the office of Public Affairs at Edwards Air Force Base provided the majority of photographs in this book. Others were provided by Marshall University in Huntington, West Virginia, the National Air and Space Museum, Smithsonian Institution, Washington, D.C., the Northrop Corporation, and the Dwight D. Eisenhower Library. The author and the editors are grateful to all these institutions for permission to print the photos in this biography of Brigadier General Charles E. Yeager.

CONTENTS

CHAPTER 1

Top Secret

It was six o'clock in the morning, and the first streaks of bright red sun were just beginning to light up the desert sky. Test pilot Chuck Yeager drove toward the Muroc Airfield Base entrance, past the sign that read: TOP SECRET.

The sign was posted because Muroc was the secret test base for the United States Air Force. It was an isolated spot, yet called "the world's finest landing field," because it was flat and spacious, so it was perfect for trying out fledgling jet planes under government security.

That morning, October 14, 1947, only a few of the men on the California base knew what was about to happen. Chuck Yeager, a captain in the Air Force, was going to fly the Bell X-1 rocket faster than any man had ever flown before. He was going to try flying it faster than the speed of sound. That meant going beyond the speed at which sound waves travel, which is 761 miles per hour at sea level. What Chuck Yeager was aiming to do was break the sound barrier!

USAF

Capt. Yeager was named project pilot of the X-1. He named the rocket and other aircraft he flew after his wife, Glennis.

As he approached the hangar he began to sense tension in the air. It almost crackled like the Mojave Desert heat at midday. Everyone knew what strange and mysterious things happened to some of the new planes when they flew into space. People sometimes imagined the sound barrier as an invisible wall of steel or brick no human could ever penetrate. Some pilots barely made it back to tell their terrifying tales of what they had experienced when they approached it. Some never made it back at all. Scientists and engineers were learning about "shock waves"—powerful speeding shells of compressed air, which under certain conditions could rip an airplane to pieces.

Chuck was well aware of these dangers. But he was a crack pilot—cool, level-headed and sure of himself. He always said you had to "know your job," and he definitely knew his. That was one of the reasons he had been chosen to pilot this secret project. And believing he was the right man for it, he had immediately said "yes."

Now Chuck entered the Air Force base hangar. There it was—the Bell X-1 rocket, the sleekest, most up-to-date aircraft designed to fly at supersonic speeds. Chuck knew every part of the tiny 31-foot-long orange and white craft, with its funny needle-shaped nose.

He had taken it up several times, first trying glide drops to give him the feel of the craft and then flying it on rocket-powered flights. He also had the best engineers and crew that a test pilot could ever hope to work with. Still, there were no guarantees he would come back alive.

After months and months of preparation, he now experienced a mixture of excitement and fear. No one knew exactly how the project would turn out; Chuck felt his "stomach trying to guess."

But there was no time to dwell on fear because Chuck and the crew had to go over the plans and details one final time. Then Chuck had to get into his pressurized suit and gloves, insulated boots and parachute.

After that the X-1 was brought out of the hangar, ready for its most daring flight ever. But of course it was not going to fly entirely on its own at the start. The rocket was far too small to hold enough fuel for both a take-off and a speed flight. The four rocket motors could carry only 288 gallons of liquid oxygen and 300 gallons of alcohol. That amount of fuel couldn't last a second more than two-and-a-half minutes. The X-1 was to be taken up in a big bomber and then dropped. That way all the fuel could be saved for the thrust to send it through that mysterious invisible wall.

The mothership chosen to carry the little rocket was the bomber craft B-29. The rocket was lowered into a concrete pit, and the B-29 was fitted over it. The bomber doors and part of the belly of the mothership had been cut away so that it could grapple the X-1 inside in just the right way to be able to release and drop it at the designated moment.

After the aircraft was fueled, Chuck and the B-29 pilot Robert Cardenas got into the big plane. They couldn't take off with Chuck in the X-1 cockpit. That would be taking one risk too many. The X-1 had no ejection seat, and if a failure or fire occurred during take-off and the rocket suddenly had to be released, the pilot would be lost with it too. Chuck would stay with Cardenas and the engineer officer, Jack Ridley, until the right time came

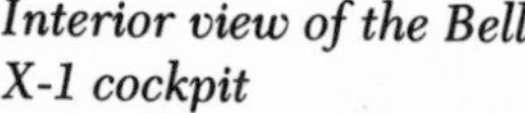

Interior view of the Bell X-1 cockpit

USAF/NATIONAL AIR AND SPACE MUSEUM, SMITHSONIAN INSTITUTION

for him to transfer to his own cockpit.

Muroc Tower cleared them, and the B-29 taxied out slowly. Then, after last-minute details, they took off suddenly in a thunderous roar, climbing at 180 miles per hour.

When they reached an altitude of 7,000 feet, Chuck was given the signal he had been waiting for. It was the moment for him to make his way into the cockpit of the aircraft cradled below. He had practiced it time after time, but it was still no easy feat.

Besides, Chuck had two broken ribs from a horseback riding accident two days earlier. He had told no one on the base about it because he knew the flight would be cancelled. Stubborn and determined to go through with his plans, the test pilot gritted his teeth every time a stab of pain shot through his chest.

The transfer was an act that could have been assigned to an acrobat. First, when Chuck went outside the mothership, he was hit by a cold lash of wind—after all, temperatures at that altitude are subfreezing. Next, he carefully treaded along a catwalk and onto a small steel ladder that dropped to the cabin door level. Unlike an acrobat or tightrope walker, he worked without a net beneath him. Then, twisting and squirming, his broken ribs aching, he managed to climb down and slip into the X-1.

Jack Ridley followed him down, lowered the door into place and locked it, sealing and pressurizing the cabin inside. Chuck felt as if he were "sealed up in a bank vault" in there. Immediately he fastened his helmet and oxygen mask. They had reached 10,000 feet by the time he made the switch, and at that altitude, his perilous climb had taken more than a normal amount of energy.

He needed oxygen badly.

The next thing Chuck did was plug in his communication system and check his instruments. There were about fifty of them, and all the equipment together weighed more than 500 pounds. They also took up every bit of space around him. In fact, the squeeze was so tight that his back rested against the liquid oxygen tank, which had a temperature of 290 degrees below zero.

Battery switch on . . . cabin pressure set . . . emergency cut-out button okay . . . finally, the entire check list completed. Now it was only a matter of time before the count-down.

Chuck had flown many experimental planes, and he had flown many dangerous aerial combat missions in Europe during World War II. But this was different. This was a venture into the unknown. And some of the many Air Force pilots who had been killed when they neared the sound barrier had been Chuck's friends. No man had dared to explore speed the way he was about to. No man had dared take that risk.

As they continued to climb, Chuck thought of his wife Glennis and their two young boys, Donald and Michael, and how much all three meant to him. While Chuck sat waiting, many thoughts of his family and his life flashed through his mind. Fear gripped him again momentarily, but he talked himself out of it. He had to maintain his concentration.

The wait seemed to last forever, but finally the countdown began. The B-29 pilot, Cardenas, called, "Five minutes to drop."

"Roger." With his jaw set tight, Chuck waited.

"Two minutes."

"Roger."

Jack Ridley asked if Chuck were still all right.

Chuck answered, taking a deep breath. "All set."

"Muroc Air Force Base to all aircraft," a Muroc Tower operator announced. "All aircraft clear. Test in progress. Repeat. All aircraft stay clear."

"Thirty seconds to drop time," Cardenas called. They were at 26,000 feet. The nose dipped, and they went into the 1,000-foot dive that preceded the release of the rocket. At fifteen seconds Chuck started his recording instruments.

"Here's your count-down. Ten-nine-eight," Cardenas said, and went on . . . "five-four-three-two-one . . . Drop!"

With a thud-like sound the X-1 was released. For a few seconds Chuck felt as if he were floating, and then, after coming out of the dark while being enclosed in the mothership, he was struck with a blinding brightness. "A fiery sun that seemed about six feet away flooded the cockpit and filled my eyes," he later remembered.

Now he leveled the plane and lit the first rocket chamber. The X-1 came alive. Then he lit the second. The plane zoomed upward, leaving the mothership behind. He lit the third. His eyes taking in everything at once and his heart almost still, Chuck Yeager readied to fire the fourth and last chamber. As he did, he spoke into the microphone attached to his helmet. "This is it," he said.

CHAPTER

2

Home in the Hills

Charles Elwood Yeager had never been inside an airplane until he went to flight school. He had never even given a thought to flying as he was growing up in a small town in the state of West Virginia. In fact, Chuck was fifteen years old the first time he ever saw an airplane. One summer afternoon some friends told him that a Beechcraft had landed in a cornfield about a mile away. So he jumped on his bike and rode out to take a look at it. "I wasn't very impressed then," he recalled years later.

Chuck was born on February 13, 1923, in the tiny town of Myra, which was situated on the upper Mud River. Within a few years he and his family moved to a modest house in nearby Hamlin. Hamlin had a population of about 500 people, but compared to Myra it seemed a real city to the young boy.

Times were tough for the Yeagers then, as they were for most people in those parts. There were days when they had to make the best of a boiled cornmeal breakfast or cornbread and buttermilk for supper. A cantaloupe or watermelon was a real treat.

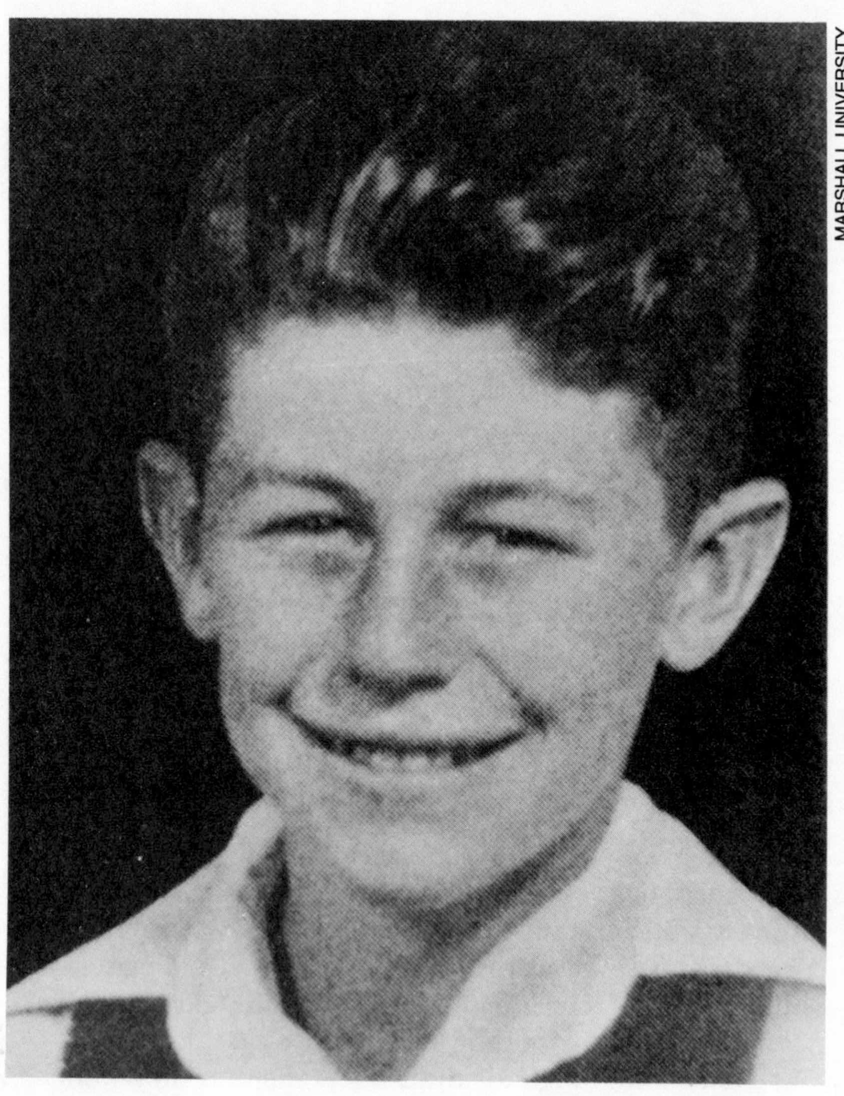

Chuck Yeager when he was growing up in Hamlin

Blue-eyed, curly-haired Chuck was the second oldest of five children. The oldest was Roy, and following Chuck were his sister Pansy Lee and his brother Hal Jr., who was ten years younger than he. Another sister, Doris Ann, died during infancy.

Chuck's father, Hal Sr., worked for a company that contracted for drilling natural gas wells throughout West Virginia and Kentucky. Because of his frequent absence from home, many of the household and farm chores fell to the children. Everyone pitched in to clean the barn and care for the chickens and pigs and the one cow they kept. Roy and Chuck sold blackberries and helped their mother Susie when she made apple butter or boiled molasses, which they used for syrup during the winter.

Chuck did his work willingly, but he preferred to run freely outdoors, climbing trees and building forts. With his friends and Roy he hunted in the backwoods, something all local folks engaged in, and fished in Mud River, where the catch was mostly bass, nabbed with grasshoppers or worms for bait.

The backwoods were a haven for Chuck. One of his close boyhood friends, Homer Hager Jr., said that Chuck "loved the hills better than anyone." He spent long hours out there, especially during the summers when he could hike and camp and climb rocks. One feat he performed particularly well was swinging through the trees like a monkey, grabbing hold of branch after branch from the top of the hill all the way down to the bottom without ever touching ground. That won him high admiration from his friends. At the swimming hole, another place where Hamlin children spent a great deal of time, Chuck was considered a good swimmer and diver as well.

Outdoor activities were mostly what the small-town young people had for recreation. Pocket money was not available to them, so they simply made the best of what they had, using their imaginations and what little materials they could scrape together. Whatever they did, they had a good time doing it.

A favorite activity was building walking stilts and challenging each other to see who could stay up on them the longest. Sometimes the stilt-walkers could last as long as three hours. Another sport was kite flying, with homemade kites.

Now and then there was a lesson to be learned from their antics. One morning Chuck and five other boys decided on a day's outing. With only a few pennies to pool among them, they bought a loaf of bread and a can of pork and beans and made a stack of pork and bean sandwiches. Then they took off on their bikes, riding to Alum Creek, a 25-mile trip. After the long ride and hours of swimming, they found themselves too exhausted to make their way home that night.

Luckily they met a family friend nearby who put them up overnight in his farmhouse. But in the morning the farmer made them work for two hours loading lumber before he would serve them any breakfast. Never had the boys earned a meal like that!

As much as Chuck loved being outdoors, which sometimes caused him to be tardy to school, he grew to enjoy other interests too. When he was in the sixth grade, a music teacher came to Hamlin and managed to convince several students to sign up to learn a musical instrument and join a drill marching band. Chuck first chose a tuba, but changed his mind and settled for the trombone, remaining a member of the band throughout his high school years. His friend Homer, who played the drums and came to be called "Drummer," later remembered Chuck as being "pretty good with that trombone," and Chuck himself admitted that he might have become somewhat of an accomplished musician if he had really put his mind to practicing.

The trombonist and the drummer put their minds and energies into the excitement of attending band festivals in other towns and meeting some new girls. At one festival some cute majorettes caught their eye, but the boys were too shy to approach them directly and ask their names. So they came up with the idea of taking pictures of the girls with an old camera they had brought along. That way they could ask the girls for their names and addresses, explaining they needed the information to send them the photos. Because the boys had no money, however, they couldn't buy film for the camera. There certainly was no need for the girls to know *that*, so it remained Chuck's and Drummer's secret.

In later years Chuck went in for basketball and finally football, which made his mother fear for his safety at every game. How could she have had any idea of the extraordinary danger her son would face when he grew up?

In school Chuck had his talents too, but he also had his troubles. He was a top geometry student, "one of the best" Gonza Methel, his math teacher, recalls ever having in her classroom. And being a mechanical expert, as he had discovered while working with automobiles and helping his dad drill in the gas fields, he found he was also a whiz at typing.

But English and history caused Chuck a struggle, and he was a daydreamer too. An elementary teacher told a magazine reporter, "The way Charlie used to sit in school daydreaming, I always suspected he had his fishing pole hidden out back somewhere. I never imagined then that he would grow up to be traveling around the country so fast."

Another teacher, Virginia Smith, who taught English, remembered that when Charlie was given a reading assignment, he took to either adventure stories or an occasional nature book. One wildlife book he read was called *Crooked-Bill, the Life of a Quail,* but when it came time to present an oral report in front of the class, Charlie was "a little bashful about it," she said.

The classroom was not the only place where Chuck and his English teacher Virginia Smith were acquainted, as often happens in a small town. The teacher's father, J.D. Smith, an attorney and former state senator, was a man with whom Chuck spent a good deal of time while his own father was away from home in the oil fields. Miss Smith said, "Charlie liked to talk man-to-man with him," especially while the retired senator was out tending his vegetable garden. "One night Dad came in to dinner, telling us he had just been out talking to Charlie," she recalled fondly. "And Charlie had announced that he wanted to be a big Army general. We all had a good laugh at that."

Later, J.D. Smith helped advise Chuck when the time came for him to make a decision about joining the Air Corps. Another military influence was an older boy named Jake Marcum. He had been Hamlin's first young resident to join the flying service in the years just before

World War II. When he returned to visit, Hamlin boys were duly impressed with him in his uniform and set of wings. One of those boys was Chuck Yeager.

By the time Chuck's high school graduation rolled around, he realized he had to seriously consider his future. He had worked for a local photographer, cleaning up the studio for five dollars a month. He had also spent many hours working on automobile engines and was recognized as an excellent mechanic. But Chuck wanted to try something new, and he wanted to see a bit of the world outside of West Virginia. Maybe, as he had told J.D. Smith, he *could* get to be "a big Army general."

When an Army Air Corps recruiter visited town, Chuck thought about applying for cadet training, but that required two years of college, which he couldn't afford. It also required a minimum age of twenty-one, and he was only eighteen. Chuck found out, though, that he could fit into another category. It was a program for enlisted pilots, asking only for a high school diploma. The plan was that he would go through flight training as an enlisted man and graduate a staff sergeant.

So in September 1941, only a few months before the Japanese attack on the American base in Pearl Harbor brought the United States into war, Chuck Yeager joined the Air Corps. Neither his teachers nor his family or friends could imagine that some day he would not only actually earn the rank of general but also make aviation history and a great contribution to science as well. Certainly Chuck himself couldn't have daydreamed anything quite like that. All he knew that fall was that he wanted to try flying. He wasn't even sure why.

CHAPTER 3

Wings

Once Chuck joined the Air Corps, he had to wait six months before he actually went up in a plane. And when he finally did, the flight went poorly for him.

His career had begun with basic training at Luke Field in Arizona, and then he was assigned to the 552nd School squadron at Victorville Army Air Base in California to learn airplane mechanics. At last one day an engineering officer invited him along on a maintenance officer flight to test an aircraft that had just been serviced. But something happened that was completely unexpected. Chuck became ill with motion sickness and threw up all over the back seat. That was mighty discouraging for someone with plans to become a pilot.

It didn't stop Chuck, though. A stubborn, willful person like him would figure a way out of that problem, and eventually he did. All he had been doing, he realized, was sitting alongside the pilot, cold and bored. As soon as he actually began to learn flying and was given a job at the controls, his stomach stopped churning. He was much too active and involved to allow any more airsickness.

At that time, "flying became fun." He understood exactly what he was doing now. He became such an accomplished mechanic, too, that in short time he was made an aviation crew chief. He had been worried about being one of the youngest trainees, but since he began to look more promising he didn't worry about that quite as much any more.

In flight school Chuck grew more eager than ever. Although he experienced the normal amount of nervousness, his first solo flight went well. Not only had he worked hard at practice, but he had rehearsed his every move over and over in his mind, a method that would serve him well later. He was proving to be an excellent student and took deep pride in his instructors' compliments.

His confidence continued to grow so quickly, in fact, that one flight instructor began to warn him against becoming a little "too cocky." Furthermore, the instructor criticized, he was displeased with the way Chuck was wearing his hat at an angle, because that was considered disrespectful by some of the other men.

Chuck wore his hat tilted down over one eye and slightly pushed up in the back. He seemed to wear it off-center purposely. As one of the enlisted men among the older, college-educated cadets, he felt that the cadets looked down on him. He knew he was just as good at the job as they were. So tipping his hat in a somewhat unacceptable manner was his way of showing how strongly he felt about himself and his own ability. But if he continued with that attitude, he was told, there was a chance he might be dropped from the program. Stiff control of behavior was a necessary part of military training.

USAF

A young Chuck Yeager in basic training

That was a time in Chuck's early career when he found himself faced with making an important decision. What *was* most important to him? he asked himself. The answer, of course: flying. After that, his attitude changed for the better.

With his basic training completed, in 1943 he was commissioned as flight officer and transferred to the 363rd Fighter Squadron, 357th Fighter Group at Tonopah, Nevada, where he went on to more advanced work in a larger aircraft. That was the Bell Aircobra, the P-39, a real fighter plane. Even though it was criticized for having problems flying at high altitude and for other difficulties with maintenance, Chuck acquired a real feel for that P-39.

With his fighter group he began learning both aerial and ground gunnery and how to fly in group formation, all difficult and demanding work. He also learned to perform aerobatics. Every now and then Chuck still tended to act a bit cocky, and of course he was as eager as ever, but now it was those qualities along with his ability that made him one of the favored pilots. Many who were found to be less skilled were dropped from the program. Some who continued, tragically, had been killed.

At Chuck's graduation, the instructor took him aside and told him something he had been wanting to hear for the last two years. "You'll make the best fighter pilot of all the cadets or students I've ever trained," he said. Now, a fighter pilot was all Chuck wanted to be. And the best, at that. He hoped his instructor's prediction was right.

As a flight officer who had earned his wings and wore

them proudly on his leather flight jacket, Chuck signed on for advanced combat training. It was the summer of 1943. The war in Europe was raging on.

Travel orders sent him as a test pilot to Wright Patterson Air Base in Ohio, which turned out to be less than 150 miles from his home in Hamlin. Early one morning Chuck got to thinking there would be nothing to it to flying over there and showing off a bit. It was seven A.M. when he flew low in a P-47 over the town, did a few rolls and came in again, skimming over the tree tops. That was called "buzzing." Later he found out that his buzzing had frightened a good many folks, especially an elderly lady who ended up in the hospital and a farmer who claimed Chuck had upset his horse while he was plowing and ruined his crop. He was sorry he had upset those people, but he still enjoyed a prank now and then.

The squadron was next based in California, near the town of Oroville. This would turn out to be an especially fortunate move for Chuck. There the men spent most of their time at work and grew closer as a fighter unit. In the evenings they sometimes went into town for a change of scene. One of their favorite places to visit was the USO, a social and recreational gathering spot for servicemen.

One night Chuck met a girl there whom he found to be as "pretty as a movie star." Her name was Glennis Faye Dickhouse. She worked as a secretary to the local school superintendent and did part-time bookkeeping work for a drug store. Pouring coffee and serving doughnuts to the servicemen at the USO was a volunteer job. She realized how homesick the men must be and how little entertainment was available for them in Oroville.

At first Glennis had trouble understanding Chuck's West Virginia accent. But Chuck made her laugh, and she found laughter a language anyone could understand. Soon they were deep in conversation, discovering how much they had in common, sharing a small-town farming background as well as an interest in horseback riding, hunting and swimming. It didn't take long before their fondness for one another grew, and they began to spend time together walking and sharing popcorn at the movies.

But Chuck was a fighter pilot now, and suddenly his squadron was being transferred, this time to Casper, Wyoming. It was hard for the young couple to say good-bye. They were afraid they might never see each other again, and neither wanted that to happen. What could they do to assure another meeting? The best arrangement they could think of was to meet in a city midway a few weeks later. They chose Reno, Nevada.

When the day came, Glennis, dressed in a new outfit and holding her train ticket in a gloved hand, arrived at the station. She found out, though, that the only train available was a freighter—and worse, she would have to ride in the caboose! It was a long, cold, lonely ride, made bearable only by the brakeman who shared his sandwich and coffee with her and, more importantly, by the thought of seeing Chuck again.

But when she arrived at the scheduled meeting place in Reno, Chuck was not there. After anxiously waiting awhile, she tried locating him at the base. Not one person she spoke to had any idea of his whereabouts. Believing that he didn't care for her any more and hadn't even taken the time to let her know, Glennis turned around and rode home. She was deeply hurt.

Meanwhile, Chuck lay in a hospital. He had bailed out of a burning plane and was found unconscious. He wasn't even supposed to have flown that day, but he had been given a last-minute assignment by a new squadron commander. There hadn't been a minute to try to contact Glennis and inform her of the plan change.

He was up there in the plane, and suddenly there was an explosion. Fire shot up from behind the seat and blew off one of the doors. He began to lose altitude quickly. There was only one thing to do—bail out! Without another moment's hesitation, he flung himself toward the door, but his helmet and mask were torn off by the rush of air. Somehow, though, he managed to double up and roll himself out.

Shakily, he reached for the parachute rip cord and pulled it, but there was more trouble. As the parachute opened, it flipped over him and knocked him out. When he regained consciousness he was in a hospital on the base. A sheepherder had found him and dragged him on a donkey to a nearby road, where he was picked up by some pilots who had seen him bail out and had sent for an ambulance.

Chuck suffered a slight concussion and a cracked vertebra, but his condition was not his first concern. He was thinking of Glennis Dickhouse and how she must have felt when he failed to show up for their date.

Of course, later she found out what had happened to Chuck, and she wrote him a letter, pouring out her feelings. Now that he was about to go overseas with the 8th Air Force, she was really full of doubts about ever seeing him again.

It was true that Chuck and the squadron were scheduled to be shipped to Europe any time, and Chuck and Glennis did manage to say good-bye in person before that day. But when she asked if there would be yet another meeting, Chuck's only answer could be, "Wait." Being a pilot or a member of a pilot's family meant waiting. Always waiting.

CHAPTER

4

Daring Escape

Chuck and the men in his squadron had spent a long time in routine classroom training. So in the winter of 1943 when they landed in England, they were ready and eager for action.

Even though he felt as prepared as he would ever be, Chuck, nevertheless, began to question himself. How would he do in combat? How would he measure up to his fellow fliers? How would he measure up against the German Nazi enemy?

But to his disappointment, there was no action for a while. The men had to return to the classroom once more to learn about new planes that were on order to be delivered. They were the P-51 Mustangs—the No. 1 American fighting aircraft of the war.

Meanwhile, Chuck and his unit idled away some of their spare hours by riding English bikes through the misty winter countryside. When it began to snow, they had to give that up.

Then in January the new aircraft finally arrived, and at last the action was about to begin. Tension filled the briefing room as the briefing officer gave instructions for the unit's first combat mission. Pointing to the maps, he warned the men of each known danger zone.

As was the situation with all of the men, Chuck felt a bit shaky. One minute he was wary of his first try at combat, but the next minute he couldn't wait to experience it. Whichever way he wavered, there was one particular thought that comforted him. He trusted his squadron buddies, with whom he had flown so many hours, and he felt a sense of safety in their company.

The young military pilot was also highly respected by the men with whom he was about to fly combat. A close squadron friend, Clarence "Bud" Anderson, later said there wasn't a pilot among them who didn't like Chuck and want to be near him during a dangerous mission. "Yeager was the best," Bud said. "No one matched his skill or courage."

It seemed natural then that Chuck be chosen to lead a flight on his first mission. As soon as he went out onto the field and saw his plane, he found a second source of comfort. He had named his plane "Glamorous Glennis" after the girl he loved who was waiting patiently for him at home.

With instructions to fly over Hamburg, Germany, first, the unit went up, but there were no German planes in sight that day. The same thing happened during the next mission and the mission after that. It only made Chuck more determined, and when at last he shot down his first German plane, he was proud that he had accomplished what he'd set out to do. He destroyed his second enemy aircraft then also—only a few minutes after his first!

That night, in the dimly lit hut where he slept, he

wrote a letter to the girl back in Oroville. " 'Glamourous Glennis' came through!" he exclaimed. Throughout his career he would name other aircraft after her, including the famous X-1 rocket.

The proud young fighter pilot started with a good record, but how long could he keep it up? Not for long, unfortunately. On his ninth mission, Chuck himself was shot down.

It happened early in the afternoon on Sunday, March 5, 1944. He was positioned at the tail end of a flight of Mustangs that had taken off from their base on the English coast, and they were flying over France, escorting B-24s on a bombing run. All of a sudden, three enemy Focke-Wulf fighters appeared on the scene. The captain leading Chuck's flight called for their planes to protect Chuck's aircraft while he tried to go after one, but when he turned from formation, one of the Focke-Wulfs hit him! To Chuck, "the world exploded."

The first thing he noticed was that his engine caught fire. Then the oxygen system blew up, leaving a big hole in the wing. Chuck knew he had to jump. He began to grope his way out, but as he tried, he gashed his head. And from the blast, his feet and hands were shot full of lead from the flak, exploding shells fired from anti-aircraft cannons. Chuck was numb, too numb to jump. Now the plane was in a steep dive. Finally he came around, and at last, at 5,000 feet, he pulled himself together, jumped and opened his chute.

The news spread quickly back in Hamlin. Friends and neighbors came to offer support to the Yeager family. Mrs. Yeager called Glennis where she was still living in Oroville and read her the telegram she had received from the War Department. It stated: "Your son Flight Officer Charles E. Yeager has been reported missing in action over the South of France . . ."

Chuck had come down in a wooded area about fifty miles south of Bordeaux. He was in pain and bleeding badly, and glad to have survived. But he quickly realized that he could not continue to survive if he stayed in the woods. The Germans knew he had been shot down; they knew the area and would be hunting for him. He could only allow himself a few minutes rest, and then he would have to drag himself to his feet and find some place to hide.

Cold and numb, Chuck huddled in the brush under his parachute. From his survival kit he pulled a chocolate bar and ate it. Then, just as he felt himself beginning to doze, he heard a noise and looked up. There he saw an elderly man standing over him. Fortunately, the man didn't appear to be German, but whispered something in French. Quickly afterward he disappeared, only to return a short time later with a woman who also spoke French and motioned for Chuck to follow them, crouching quietly through the brush. Who were these people? Where were they leading him? Whatever they were doing, Chuck realized that they were taking a dangerous chance with their own lives. France was occupied by the Germans, and the three of them by now were completely surrounded by German patrols.

Hastily, these strangers pushed Chuck into a nearby barn, which was dark and airless, and up into a hayloft above. "Silence, silence," they whispered, and again quickly rushed away, leaving Chuck alone once more.

From outside Chuck heard the harsh sounds of German voices. Closer and closer they approached. Like a small animal, Chuck burrowed himself into the haystack. Not surprisingly, then, the barn door opened, and heavy, booted footsteps trampled across the floor and began climbing the ladder to the loft. Deep under the hay Chuck huddled, still as stone. He felt the hay rustle all around him as a bayonet poked on one side of him and then the other. It seemed a miracle that it missed his body.

Until they left, Chuck's heart pounded furiously, and it continued hammering for a long time afterward. He couldn't help but think about war and question the meaning of why human beings fought one another the way they did.

It was only when the French man and woman returned and whispered to him that he dared to move. Choked, dusty and caked with dried blood, he crawled out and allowed himself to be led from the barn.

The woman introduced herself as Madame Latrielle and her father as Bertrand. Her husband, she explained, was taken prisoner of war by the Germans. Before they could help Chuck, though, they had to do something important, and for this they apologized. They had to take him to an English-speaking woman who could question him to make sure he was an American and not a spy. In wartime, they said, you could never be too careful about whom you trusted. The Germans wouldn't spare anyone who aided an American flier and would shoot them all mercilessly on the spot.

The woman Chuck was brought before was named Madame Starodvorsky, and she had learned English from a governess when she was a girl. Now she lay in bed ill with rheumatism. She found the pilot to be, amazingly, "just a boy." But she thoroughly grilled him until she felt satisfied that he was telling the truth.

Next Chuck was taken by his rescuers to their farmhouse kitchen, where Madame Latrielle cut off his boots and bathed his injuries. Then he was served a bowl of soup, a chunk of bread and some cheese, his first meal in a long while. Immediately afterward he was sneaked back into the barn, where a village doctor paid him a short visit, picking the shrapnel out of his hands and feet and tending a leg wound.

His wounds were the least of his troubles, the doctor told Chuck before departing. If Chuck were to come out of this ordeal alive, he was going to have to make his way into Spain, a safe territory because it was a neutral country at the time. The 100-mile trip through German-occupied France and over the steep Pyrenees Mountains into the safety of Spain would be a dangerous one every step of the way, because the Germans would never give up hunting him. And certainly Chuck was in no condition to walk that distance anyway. But he couldn't stay indefinitely with this good French family and endanger their lives.

The escape proved to be a long and harrowing one, more than a young, tough, American boy could ever have imagined. First the family bravely hid Chuck for two days and nights while he regained some strength and his wounds began to heal. Then they dressed him to look like a Frenchman, in a simple jacket, dark baggy pants and a blue beret. Afterward they gave him a cross-cut woodman's saw so it would appear as if he had a purpose in being out on the road. Then they set him upon a bicycle, alongside a man who was a stranger to him, and bid him good-bye.

The stranger was part of the "underground," a system of people who worked secretly helping Americans, other allied troops and Jewish victims of the German Nazis to escape. This was only the beginning for Chuck.

Spain was far off, and he had a long way to travel. As they moved on slowly, he kept imagining that he heard the dreaded click of a bayonet, a click that could actually happen at any time.

At last, after two wearisome days on the road, hardly daring to stop for a bite of food or a moment of rest, Chuck was taken to another farmhouse and after that to still a third. This one was located in a village called Nérac. It belonged to a young couple and their little boy with the last name of Gabriel. They took Chuck in, and, because their house was visible on the main road, they hid him in a back shed, where he stayed for several days.

One day, restless and bored, Chuck decided to sit outside a bit, stretch and breathe in some fresh air, when all of a sudden a band of German soldiers came marching down the road right in front of him. It wasn't until they disappeared from view that Chuck realized what he had done by making himself so visible.

When Chuck was safely back inside, M. Gabriel scolded him severely, while his wife Marie Rose sat weeping, first with terror and then with relief. A friend of M. Gabriel, Dr. Henri, also reminded Chuck again that if he had been discovered, they all would have paid the penalty with instant death.

When the time came to leave and continue on the escape route, it was Dr. Henri who accompanied Chuck.

Toward the end of this part of the journey they rode in the back of a truck, and Chuck was dropped off at a designated spot in the dark woods. There he was introduced to three other Americans also hoping to make their way into Spain. They were further aided by British airmen who dropped bundles of food, weapons and clothing onto open fields in the middle of the night.

Cold and wet, exhausted and hungry, and always hearing that imagined click of the German bayonet, Chuck moved on with the others. Sometimes they were lucky enough to land another truck ride, but when they didn't they stumbled forward or crawled to make sure they kept out of sight. At last they arrived at the foot of the snow-covered Pyrenees Mountains. The mountains rose some 10,000 feet at their highest peaks. Even for a boy from the hills of West Virginia, the Pyrenees were awesome. The important thing for Chuck at that time, though, was knowing that on the other side of them was Spain. The date was March 23. So far Chuck had been on this perilous journey nearly three weeks.

In a tiny, hidden shack, a guide met them and gave them their final instructions. No talking. No fires. Don't forget that the most dangerous part still lies ahead of you, he explained solemnly, and then told them he estimated they could make it over the mountains in five, maybe four, days. With luck.

There was one last warning he had to give them before leaving. If they were caught, he said firmly, they must insist that they found the way by themselves. They must never let anyone know that the underground had aided them, or the network of the secret movement would be discovered and destroyed.

Chuck and his companions remained in the shack until nightfall, when they figured it was the right time to move out. Hour after hour during the first day, then the second and the third, they climbed and crawled and occasionally rested. They were hungry, numb with cold and pain, worrying now about frostbite. Two of the men fell far behind, but Chuck and the fourth man, Pat, kept going. At last on the fourth day Chuck and Pat reached the top of a ridge, found a lumberman's cabin and took shelter there, hoping for a short rest.

But as they were sleeping, Germans fired on them right through the front door, in a surprise attack. In an instant Chuck and Pat leaped through a back window, spun about in the snow and splashed into a creek, which turned out to be deep enough to keep them out of sight for a few minutes. As soon as they surfaced, though, Chuck saw that during the shelling, Pat had been hit. To Chuck's horror he saw further that one of Pat's lower legs was dangling. It hung, connected only by a tendon.

Pat urged Chuck to go on and leave him behind. But Chuck couldn't do it. He was a man who acted in an emergency, and if ever there was an emergency, it was now. With brave calm, Chuck snatched the penknife from his survival kit and cut the tendon of the half-severed leg, actually performing an amputation. Then he took a shirt that Marie Rose Gabriel had sewn for him from his parachute and wound it as a tourniquet tightly about the leg stump to stop the major bleeding. Finally, dragging the wounded man, he set out for the border. Sometimes he pushed him and sometimes he pulled him with his hands locked under Pat's arms and around his chest.

The biting cold, the sheer exhaustion, and always the nervous, keen ear of the hunted forced Chuck to stop and catch his breath more and more often. They were slowing down, and with every stop he wondered if Pat were going to die in his arms. He wondered too if he himself might actually die.

Then, unbelievably, there it was—the slope the guide had described. It was the border. They were safe! Chuck hauled Pat one last time to the edge and shoved the nearly dead man down, watching him roll, before gliding down behind him. He did this over and over until they were both at the bottom near the road.

Strangers had helped save Chuck's life, and now he had done the same for another man. It was an act that later won Chuck a Bronze Star and a citation that read: "For heroism displayed while in enemy-occupied Continental Europe."

Chuck was sure the Spanish border guards would get medical aid for the wounded man, so he left Pat where he could easily be seen. In a short time Pat was picked up and transported to a hospital where he was cared for until he recovered enough to return home.

As for himself, Chuck had no idea what the guards would do with him. He was afraid they couldn't be trusted. He was right: they couldn't be. As soon as they found the bedraggled young American, they locked him up in jail.

CHAPTER

5

Flying High Again

Chuck wasn't a criminal, and he didn't belong in a village jail. He belonged in a warm, comfortable bed following a good hot meal and a bath.

Luckily the police had not bothered to search him. He still had his survival kit in his possession, and inside it was a saw. It was a small one, but it had shark-tooth-sharp blades, and it was Chuck's only hope for getting out. So as soon as he was left alone in his cell, he sawed his way through bars that were not very strong, found a place with rooms to rent and fell into a deep sleep.

Chuck spent six weeks in Spain, lying in the sun and regaining lost weight while the American Consul worked at releasing him and five other American airmen who also had been shot down. Finally, he was returned to England, where immediately he was taken to Supreme Headquarters Allied Expeditionary Forces (SHAEF). At the headquarters he was asked question after question. Name. Rank. Age. Exactly what happened to his plane? How was he shot down? How did he escape being captured by the Germans? What German troops saw him? What was the troop's size? Who helped him in the French underground network?

The interrogators spread a map on a table before him. It was a map of the area surrounding Angouleme, where he had come down, and he was requested to point out each spot, relay what took place there to the best of his memory and point out the route he traveled as well as each place he stayed along the way. The questioning went on for an entire day.

Chuck understood the importance of SHAEF knowing every detail of what had happened in order to learn how much information the enemy might have gained about the allied countries in combat against the Germans. Because of this, Chuck answered patiently, often repeating the same statements over and over.

Chuck was relieved when the interrogation finally ended. But one of the men had some bad news for him. Chuck thought he would be able to return immediately to his squadron, and, in fact, he looked forward to nothing else. That was not to be, he was told. Instead he was going to have to go back to the United States. In fact, flight arrangements had already been made for the middle of June, which was only weeks away. He would return briefly to his squadron and then fly directly to New York.

"Back to the States?" he asked, shocked. "No way!" What could he do for the war effort back there!

Sorry, but those were the rules, he was told. He was now called an "evadee." He had evaded, or escaped, the Germans, and he had received help from the French underground. That meant he knew so much about the underground workings that his knowledge could be extremely dangerous. If he returned to fighting, he took the chance of being captured. Then in the most brutal way the Germans could force the detailed information out of him and end up killing him as well as every person who had aided him along the way. Of course, the rule made sense to Chuck.

But back in his bunk that night, he tried to think of a way to comfort himself, convincing himself that rules are rules and that's the way it goes in wartime. On the other hand, he thought of his former squadron roommate who had been killed recently and about how the two of them and all their buddies were so tightly joined together in this war mission. All he wanted was to get back to the job he had started out to do. He just wasn't ready to go home. Not yet.

In his autobiography *Yeager*, written with author Leo Janos, Chuck wrote, "I figured the war had been cut out from under me before I could make worthwhile all those hard and expensive months of combat training. There wasn't a rule ever invented that couldn't be bent. So I marched on group headquarters and began my fight."

Chuck went from colonel to general, pleading his case. By June he knew that the Allies were about to begin a new invasion, and they needed all the valuable men they could get. One general listened to his arguments and finally said, "I think Ike would like to meet you."

Ike was General Dwight D. Eisenhower, the Supreme Commander of the Armed Forces, who some years after the war was elected president of the United States. When Chuck told the Supreme Commander his story and how he still had a "lot of fighting left to do," General

Eisenhower nodded sympathetically, yet insisted he didn't have the authority to keep Chuck in combat duty because the regulation was the War Department's and not his. He promised, however, that he would call Washington, D.C., and ask that special permission be granted in this case.

In the meantime, Chuck gladly rejoined his group, but the squadron commander told him that until the answer came from Washington, Chuck was only allowed to fly noncombat. Impatient and restless, Chuck watched his friends go out on missions and listened to their animated conversations when they returned. He was eager to hear about everything that happened, but he felt very much left out.

Then one day he was in the air over the British base when an operations officer radioed to him. The officer had just heard from Air Sea Command, he explained, and had learned that a B-17 was ditched off the coast of Holland. Furthermore, he went on, he had decided to send three planes to rescue the crew. Would Chuck watch after them? the officer asked.

Glad to have something to do, Chuck agreed and immediately turned in the direction of Holland. He guided the other planes in a search until he finally came across the crew bobbing in a dinghy in the water below. He was circling when all of a sudden he sighted a German JU-88, a Junkers patrol bomber.

Forgetting about the fact that he was still considered grounded and not allowed to engage in combat, the impulsive Chuck signaled the other three planes. He wanted to get that Junker, and he turned and went after it, firing and blowing it to pieces.

Back at the base, the commanding officer was furious. Chuck had been restricted to flying over his British base, and now not only had he flown over the English Channel, he had gone ahead on his own and shot down a plane. The officer was especially angry because he would have to answer for the action since he had been the one to send Chuck out on the rescue in the first place.

Luckily for Chuck, though, the commander settled the matter quietly. Then at last the long-awaited answer from Washington came through. Eisenhower had been granted the authority to make the decision, and he gave the determined and headstrong Yeager permission to return to combat.

Once again Chuck was a fighter pilot. He was a part of Fighter Group 357, which was made up of three squadrons. Returning to his group and going back to his job gave him a feeling he would never forget. The men who had survived—for many had lost their lives—had become so close in friendship that Chuck was at a loss for words to describe it.

In his autobiography, Chuck talked about character development and how fast he and the other young fighter pilots grew up during wartime. Maybe it was good and maybe it was bad, but one thing those men could say with pride was that they learned how to use their skills and handle themselves in danger. They had a job, and they did it.

The following fall Chuck was chosen to lead a number of missions and then was assigned as a group leader to lead all three squadrons on a bomber escort mission. Before he knew it he was promoted to captain, and not only was he flying, he had become squadron maintenance officer, with the job of checking out all the overhauled Mustangs. At the time he was not quite twenty-two years old.

Anyway, the war was winding down. Chuck was flying his last missions, writing to Glennis, and giving some thought to the future.

When the war did end and Chuck left Europe with his squadron, his record showed that he had flown sixty-four combat missions and a total of 270 combat hours and had officially shot down fourteen planes. He had become a double-ace (a record of shooting down five planes earned a pilot the title of "ace"), and he had become a real hero back in Hamlin, where he was given a parade and a rousing reception in the gym of his old high school.

In addition to the Bronze Medal he had won for heroism in saving the life of his wounded comrade, Pat, he was awarded the Distinguished Flying Cross "for extraordinary achievement while serving as a fighter pilot on an escort mission over Germany." He also received the Silver Star for shooting down five Messerschmitt 109s on one mission, and a Silver Star Cluster for shooting down four Focke-Wulf 190s on another. Then he earned the Distinguished Flying Cross Air Medal for aerial achievement and the Purple Heart for wounds received in action. Furthermore, a Presidential Unit Citation was presented to the 357th Squadron for extraordinary achievement while flying combat in the European theatre.

Just as planned, Chuck and Glennis had waited for each other. Immediately upon Chuck's return to the

United States, he headed for Oroville and announced to Glennis that he wanted to take her home to meet his folks. When they arrived in Hamlin, the war hero and his bride-to-be were greeted by the entire town and given a big celebration. Chuck was a hero, but he didn't like to brag about it. People found him much the same fellow he always was, a bit mischievous, still a "tease," according to his mother, and a "good hometown boy," according to his friend, Homer.

On February 26, 1945, Chuck and Glennis were married in the Yeager family home. The parlor was stuffed full of flowers, and a beautiful altar was fashioned and decorated as well. Chuck's older brother Roy was in the Navy and was not able to get back to Hamlin, but the rest of his family was there. So was J.D. Smith, Chuck's friend who had helped advise him with his military career.

Following a two-week California beach honeymoon, Chuck and Glennis went to Perrin Field in Texas, where Chuck was assigned as a pilot instructor. After the action in Europe and the sense of importance he held there, this seemed a tame assignment, and it made him grumble. He couldn't wait for it to end.

Not long after that assignment began, the military set up a new regulation that allowed prisoners of war and evadees back in the United States to choose their assignments. With Glennis expecting their first child, Chuck chose the base closest to Hamlin so his family could help. That returned him to Wright Field in Ohio.

"The fact that this was the center for flight testing didn't occur to me," he said. "When I reported and they saw from my records that I had about 1,100 hours of flying time, had a maintenance background, and had been a crew chief, they decided to put me in the Flight Test Division as an assistant maintenance officer."

But Chuck Yeager was not to stay on the ground for long. The work at Wright was going to take him to Muroc Air Base where he would face the most exciting and challenging assignment of his career.

CHAPTER

6

The Invisible Wall

When Chuck arrived at Muroc in 1946, it was a place unlike any he'd been assigned to before. In the midst of the California high desert, it was barren and desolate. Cactus and crooked Joshua trees dotted the area, and layers of red dust blew with gusty winds up to sixty-five miles an hour. Almost everything was faded from the sun or pitted from the sand. During the day the temperature climbed to a high of 120 degrees. At night it dropped rapidly. Winter temperatures fell below zero.

Housing for the most part consisted of made-over barracks or tumbledown shacks. With no comfortable housing available for a married couple, Chuck and Glennis were forced to separate once again. Glennis lived in Hamlin, and for a long while they would have to settle for a less than idealistic arrangement.

Even though Muroc was in the midst of a barren desert, there was one thing that made it a perfect test area. That was the ideal terrain of the landing field, Rogers Dry Lake, a lake bed of solid clay—smooth, level and hard. It was seven miles long and five miles wide.

Chuck came to Muroc from Wright, where he had become an outstanding test pilot. There at Muroc he flew some eight hours daily, flying every kind of plane available, including captured German and Japanese planes. One was even the Focke-Wulf 190, just like the one that had shot him down over France.

Nobody had logged more flying time than Chuck at Wright, and nobody had liked climbing into an airplane cockpit and continually learning more than he did. He also liked everything there was to like about working with engines and gadgets and figuring out exactly how they functioned. What a perfect combination for a crackerjack experimental test pilot!

The chief of Muroc's flight test division, Colonel Alfred G. Boyd, liked the way Chuck flew. A short time after Chuck's arrival, Col. Boyd assigned him and another combat pilot Bob Hoover, who had also been shot down, to perform in air shows across the country. Not much of the American public had seen jet planes yet.

Then in the spring of that year a rumor spread across the base. It was whispered that the Air Force might head a project—one that involved assigning a military pilot to fly a new rocket. The project was to determine if that rocket could fly as fast as the speed of sound.

Sound travels at 761 miles per hour at sea level, but decreases to about 660 miles per hour above 45,000 feet, since sound travels slower in colder air. Man had never before reached that speed, which was being measured with a Mach number (named after Ernst Mach, the Austrian physicist who devised the system). The Muroc airmen who were talking about the new rocket referred to the term Mach 1, a transsonic speed equal to the speed of sound.

The project was being developed by Bell Aircraft Corporation under the direction of the National Advisory Committee for Aeronautics. Now that the war was over and attention could be turned to new aviation advances, the corporation's president, Lawrence Bell, hoped to meet the challenge of developing an aircraft that would fly at speeds near 1,600 or 1,700 miles per hour and climb to altitudes of 80,000 feet. The project was a multimillion-dollar flying research laboratory. It was called the Bell X-1.

Begun in 1943, it was designed not only to explore critical speeds in the transsonic range (600–900 miles per hour) and supersonic range (900 miles per hour and beyond), but also to record the activities of the mysterious, turbulent and dangerous forces out there. This was an important step in exploring space. Space begins in the ionosphere, at an altitude of 120 miles, where the air is so thin that resistance to a moving object stops, and the only force slowing its speed is gravity thousands of miles out from earth.

Two important questions were being asked. One, was it possible for a straight-wing airplane to fly faster than the speed of sound? Two, if that were possible, could a pilot ever control the violent battering and buffeting the plane and pilot suffered at such incredible speeds?

The problems seemed to be caused by a force called "shock waves." Toss a stone into a pool of water, and you will see waves ripple outward. Throw a ball or fly a model plane, and you will create invisible air vibrations. The waves you send out into the air with the ball or plane prepare the air ahead, you might say, for the movement of the objects. A bullet rushes into the air one way as it pushes the gun in the opposite direction

Sound Waves

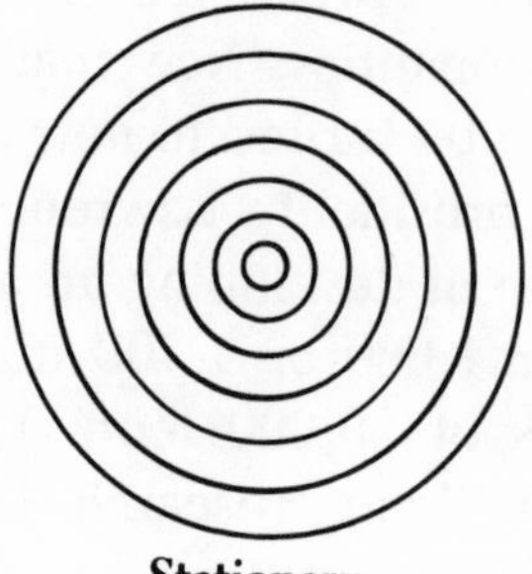

Stationary

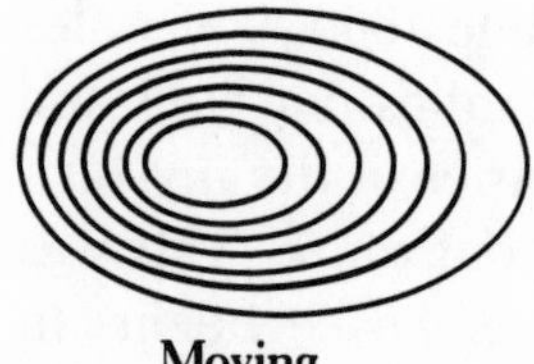

Moving

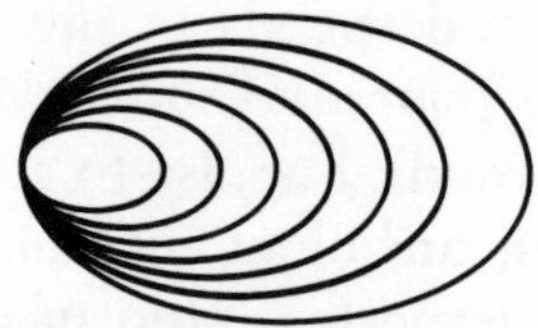

Moving at
Sonic Speed

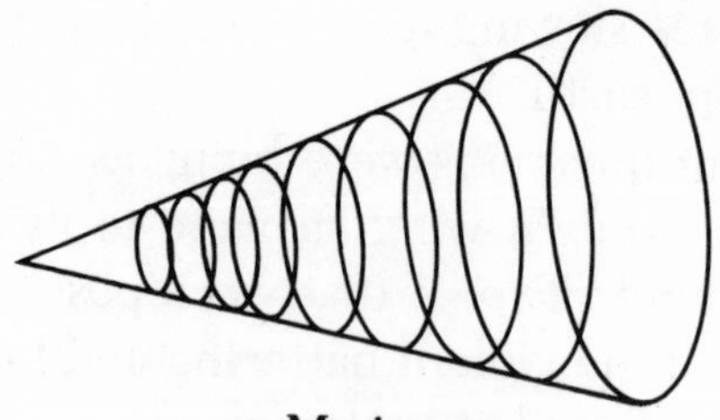

Moving at
Supersonic Speed

with an equal amount of pressure. It was Sir Isaac Newton who discovered the law of motion that every action going in one direction creates an equal reaction moving in the opposite direction.

An airplane in motion sends out sound-carrying waves. When the air flows around the plane, pressure disturbances are created in the air. A plane flying at a slower speed can prepare the air waves and have a smooth ride. But if it travels at supersonic speed, the pressure disturbances build up and lock together so tightly that they form shock waves. Flying faster than the speed of sound, then, would mean that the plane is traveling faster than the speed at which its disturbances can travel. Those shock waves attach themselves to the front and rear of the plane. That is what twisted and pounded and buffeted the airplanes that test pilots had been experiencing so far.

Scientists and engineers working in laboratories and gigantic wind tunnels were only beginning to understand the problems created by shock waves. They still hadn't realized exactly what that dreaded "wall" or "sound barrier" was. There actually was neither. Instead, it was the point in flight when the speed of the plane matched the speed of the sound waves sent out by the plane in all directions.

Many men working on the X-1 were convinced that breaking through that "wall" or flying at Mach 1 was impossible. Some disagreed. One of those men who believed that it could be done was Col. Boyd.

The rocket rumor on the base turned out to be true. The Air Force and Col. Boyd had definitely decided to take on the X-1.

Now it was time to choose the pilot. Although experimental flying is described as lonely work, thousands of pilots wanted to go into testing. But the list of requirements was long and rigid, so there were not many more than 125 test pilots at Muroc. Many of them volunteered for the new project.

There followed days and nights of talk and decision making. Finally the field was narrowed down to two men. The second would be the backup man. The first choice was Captain Charles E. Yeager.

Col. Boyd reasoned that Chuck was the right selection because of "his demonstrated outstanding ability as a pilot, his obvious stability, reliability and determination." Chuck was called into the colonel's office for an interview with him and one of his deputies.

"What would you do if you were the pilot assigned?" the deputy asked Chuck.

"Sir, I'd start with a great deal of care," Chuck replied. "With so much at stake I'd proceed very cautiously."

Then Col. Boyd asked him, "Do you think an aircraft can fly at sonic speed?"

"Yes, Sir," Chuck answered. "I've fired many a rifle, Colonel. Even a 22-caliber bullet travels at faster than the speed of sound. You can fire into the water, which is much denser than air, and the bullet is not distorted by speed alone. There may be other factors involved in the flight of an airplane. But that speed itself is no insurmountable obstacle. If you take it a little bit at a time."

Colonel Boyd remained silent for a moment. Then solemnly he reminded Chuck that nobody would ever really know what happens at Mach 1 until somebody was able not only to get there, but also to get back. "This is an extremely risky mission," he said.

There followed more talk, more questions. Chuck grew tense. He knew what question was coming next, and it was going to require a good deal of deep thought and decision making.

Then finally Col. Boyd asked Chuck if he wanted the assignment.

Chuck's immediate gut reaction was to say "yes." But there was so much more to consider. His family was very important to him, and he held a strong sense of responsibility toward them. Glennis was living in Hamlin with their son Donald and a new baby, Michael, and although by telephone she said she would approve of whatever decision he reached, it was still a tough one. There were his parents to think of too. And why, he asked himself squarely, should any man take such a risk at all? He would receive no extra pay for it, and if he made it to Mach 1 and back, he would be in the public eye and would no longer have much privacy in his life.

On the other hand, it was a chance of a lifetime to make a breakthrough in man's never-ending quest to explore the unknown, to go faster than any living being. He also had confidence in himself as well as that of his commanding officer.

The project engineer, Richard Frost, believed in him too. "Charlie Yeager is the coolest guy I've ever seen," Frost said, "and it's my business to see a lot of pilots preparing for flights of doubtful outcome. He is a perfectly natural airman . . . he flies a plane as if it were part of him. In his test work he does exactly what the aeronautical engineers request, and he brings back the answers."

USAF/NATIONAL AIR AND SPACE MUSEUM, SMITHSONIAN INSTITUTION

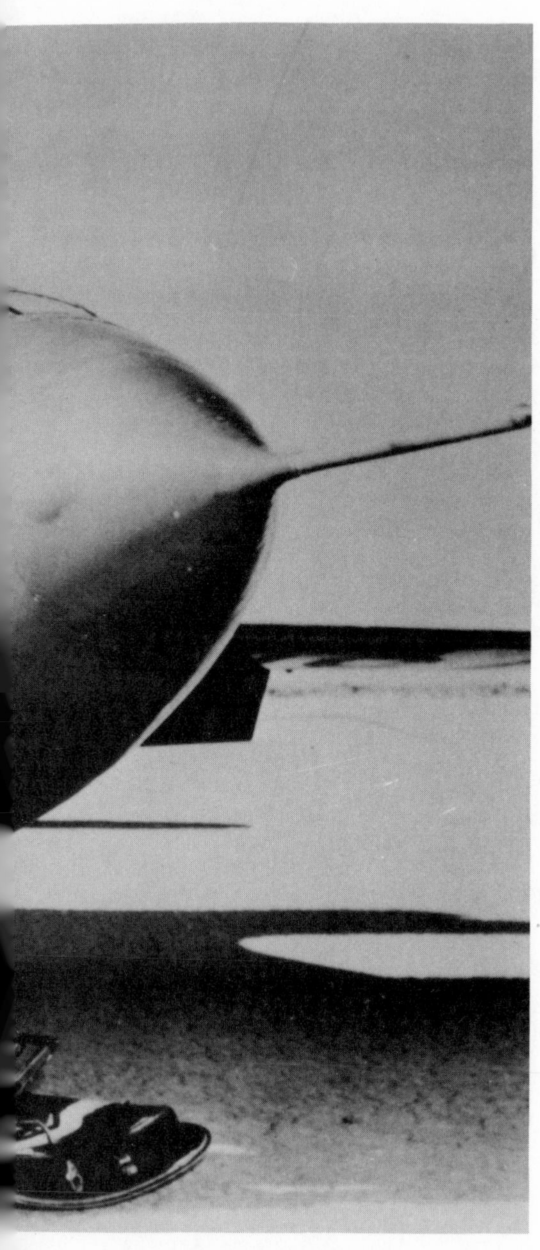

Capt. Yeager climbs into the X-1, showing the small size of the rocket. His friend, Jack Ridley (center) and a Bell Company mechanic look on.

Chuck went out to the hangar to take a close look at the X-1, which was fastened down inside it. He climbed into the cockpit and fired the engines. As he explained it, "a sheet of flame shot twenty feet out the back door," and at that moment he heard "the loudest man-made noise ever heard on earth."

To Chuck, it was the most impressive airplane he had ever seen. At last he answered Col. Boyd's question.

"Yes, I believe I could do it," he said. "I would like to try, Sir."

It was back to the classroom for Chuck. There was a great deal to learn about the Bell X-1, and one good way to begin was by studying the model. The X-1 was designed, of course, to withstand shock waves and to make air flow smoothly over it. It was built to hold up under forces eighteen times the pull of gravity, making it the most rugged airframe ever constructed at that time. The wings were short and stubby, yet extremely strong to manage the heavy weight of the craft. Each part was designed with balance and control in mind. The fuselage, the plane's body, was streamlined, yet it had to be rounded enough to carry fuel. To keep the bullet shape of the forward fuselage, the cockpit canopy was devised as part of the fuselage decking.

The fuel system was carefully selected—liquid oxygen (called "lox") and alcohol. They were easy to get, had good power potential, and were generally safe to handle by the ground crew. With this fuel system and the design of the rocket engines, each rocket chamber produced 1,500 pounds of engine thrust, giving the rocket motor thrust a total of 6,000 pounds.

Even paint was given special consideration. The combination of friction heat and outer subzero temperatures caused the paint to crack, so specific mixed lacquers were used. Twenty coats of them!

Chuck trained with backup pilot Bob Hoover, his friend from Wright Patterson. The two men had developed a deep admiration and respect for each other. Together they "stepped into the unknown," testing newly designed high-altitude pressure suits, getting locked into sealed chambers and being strapped into centrifuges, fast-rotating machines used to test their ability to withstand gravitational forces. They also were subjected to tough physical stamina tests that sometimes made them sick to their stomachs. These were the first tests of this kind and eventually led the way to methods of testing and preparation for astronauts before their first flights into space.

Another important crew member was engineering officer Jack Ridley, a small but wiry man who had been a wrestling champion in college. Chuck admired and respected him too and often remarked that he trusted Jack enough to put his life into Jack's hands. He called Jack "the brain behind the project."

Classroom lessons and question sessions went on hour after hour, day after day. Being back in a classroom situation, though, brought out some of Chuck's old self-conscious feelings about lacking a college education. And those feelings brought out that sense of competitiveness in him again.

But Dick Frost, the project engineer, had been highly

USAF/NATIONAL AIR AND SPACE MUSEUM, SMITHSONIAN INSTITUTION

The Bell rocket shown beneath a B-50 aircraft on lifts. The B-50 was the mothership which carried the X-1A

impressed with Chuck from the start. He thought that for Chuck to wonder if he were as good as the college graduates was nonsense. Frost saw that whenever he lectured or drew diagrams, Chuck's eyes showed clearly that he understood and absorbed everything. Instantly Frost realized how capable Chuck was and how much "the guy was an instinctive engineer."

The first actual practice flight was a nonpowered glide flight. The X-1 was dropped without power rather than flown with the lox and alcohol. Even though it was a nonpowered flight, there was still so much excitement in the air about it that Chuck admitted he could hardly eat breakfast that morning. Chuck rode the B-29 with the X-1 grappled underneath in the bomb bay until they reached the designated altitude. Then, as rehearsed on the ground, he made his way along the catwalk and down the ladder into the X-1 cockpit. There he waited until they climbed to the next designated altitude level and received the signal announcing his glide drop.

"The first drop was quite an experience for me," Chuck wrote in a book called *Plane Talk*. "You are sitting there. It is quite dark. The bomber pilot says, 'I'll give you a five-minute warning here, and you can set up and set in and get a death grip on the stick.' He gives you about a minute warning and then he starts counting down to five seconds and he says five seconds, four, three, two, one, drop and the co-pilot finally releases you.

"When you fall out, it comes out with a snap, and the bright sunlight blinds you quite severely for a matter of two or three seconds until you become acclimatized to the light."

It was a silent, graceful ride, and when he landed and climbed out, he announced he had just experienced the "best darned plane" he had ever flown.

With each following run, Chuck familiarized himself more with the rocket, developing a better and better feel for it and an even stronger faith in its equipment. His excitement and enthusiasm reached new heights as well. Every motion of the run was perfected. For one, Chuck learned to make sure his oxygen mask was in perfect shape. There was no oxygen backup system, and once he was given a leaky mask and ended up dizzy and light-headed. He also learned to keep his helmet inside the X-1 cockpit so he wouldn't have to hang onto it during his tricky cockpit transfer.

Nonpowered flights were great, but Chuck was anxious to zoom ahead. He knew how foolish it would be, though. He knew the only way to come through the experiment alive was to take it step by step as he had claimed at the start.

In the middle of his rigorous practice schedule, he took a break and returned to Hamlin to pick up Glennis and the children and bring them out to the California base. For the first time Glennis saw the dusty, desolate Muroc where her husband had been living. It was far from any kind of place a young couple would like to raise a family. But at least Chuck and Glennis were together again for a while. Furthermore, she had arrived just in time for Chuck's first powered flight, which took place on August 28, 1947.

Everyone admitted nervousness, including the X-1 pilot himself. But as long as he was busy detailing, he was able to put his jitters aside. During the ride up, shackled under the B-29, he sat in the dark and cold, waiting. Waiting was always one of the hardest parts.

Chuck was supposed to simply "feel out the engine" on this flight. He was not supposed to go the limit, as fast as the speed of sound, but only approach it. He was to reach the speed of Mach .8, or 80 percent of the speed of sound.

That was easier said than done, however. Nearing the planned speed, he found the sensation of high-speed flying so fantastic that he couldn't seem to stop himself from getting carried away. Leaving the limits of the known world and "stepping into the unknown" was more glorious than he had ever dreamed. What a plane! What a flight!

Suddenly he realized he was moving beyond the arranged speed for this trial run. Quickly he shut everything off. Then he glided back down and came in for a landing.

He had caused some tense moments because of his excitement and enthusiasm. After a few strong words from Col. Boyd, Chuck promised to follow each scheduled flight step by step from then on so all the rocket data could be properly analyzed. After all, there was no such thing as a computer then. The "computer" back in those early days of experimental rocket flying was the pilot himself.

On the second powered flight, Chuck took the airplane up to a little higher speed, and for the first time he experienced that dreaded buffeting. Shock waves had formed at the thick part of the wing, resulting in terrifying, violent turbulence.

With each practice flight, he "kicked it up" a little

higher. Once he went up to Mach .94, or 94 percent of the speed of sound, but that time something went wrong. When he pulled on the control column, the airplane did not turn, but just kept going the direction it was headed. So he shut everything off and came back down to begin work on ironing out that problem.

Another problem developed with frost forming on the windshield, but that was solved with an unusual solution that cost only a few dollars. Someone had the idea of applying a coating of shampoo to the windshield as an antifrost, and it worked, although no one was able to explain exactly how.

Eventually, all the problems were solved. The next step was taking the tiny, powerful rocket all the way up to Mach 1. At last Chuck and the crew were ready to go for it!

CHAPTER

7

The "Sound Barrier"

It was a tense moment when Chuck fired the fourth and last rocket on that momentous October day in 1947. The X-1 blazed forward with a mighty roar. Its thrust came on so fast and so powerful that it forced Chuck backward with an alarming jolt. Momentarily he could hardly reach his hands out toward the controls.

Speed itself doesn't cause man harm, but a forceful slowing or acceleration of body motion can. When a pilot's body is suddenly accelerated upward or forward, blood is forced away from the head and into the abdomen and legs. This deprives the brain of blood, and the result could be deadly. Fortunately that didn't happen to Chuck. All precautions had been taken. He sat in a pressurized cabin, maintained near sea-level air pressure, even though he was flying at high altitudes where the air was thin. He wore a pressurized helmet, which sent oxygen into his breathing passages, continually charging his lungs. And he also wore an anti-G (gravity) suit, built to inflate automatically in an emergency, in order to squeeze the body and prevent the rapid blood rush.

Recomposed after the jolt, Chuck turned his attention toward the Machmeter. It was getting closer and closer to Mach 1. The heavy, horrifying buffeting began. It felt as if giant sledgehammers were pounding the aircraft all around him in wildly rapid succession. It gave him the sensation that the plane was being twirled and twisted until nothing would be left of it.

As Chuck believed, you had to "know your job," and with his thorough knowledge and vast experience, he was able to keep the plane from flipping over or going into a dive. He knew exactly how to handle the craft. Even when the plane began losing stability, he managed to keep the upper hand.

The Machmeter now indicated .96—96 percent there. At that instant, the needle began to flicker. The next thing Chuck knew, the needle had gone right off the scale!

"It's gone screwy!" he cried as he radioed to Ridley in the B-29, and that seemed to be all he could say.

When that happened, the buffeting disappeared too. Now all of a sudden the ride was strangely and unbelievably smooth. It was almost silent.

"I was so high and so remote, and the airplane was so very quiet that I might have been motionless," Chuck later recalled.

He was alone with the incredible sensation of perhaps shooting for the moon or the stars or another planet—out there in a layer of thin atmosphere. This made him the first real space man.

The "impossible" had happened. Captain Charles E. Yeager, a man of courage and faith in both himself and in science and technology, had flown in front of the sound waves and left them all behind the Bell X-1 rocket. He had flown faster than the speed of sound! The day he "smashed" through what was thought to be an invisible barrier out there in the sky was the day he opened a new era of exploration. Breaking the record was not significant by itself alone. Shirley Thomas, author of *Men of Space*, explained that it "opened the skies to speeds that men had feared would never be reached, and once Yeager had shattered that imaginary sonic barrier, the whole infinity of the universe was suddenly within reach of man."

Meanwhile, as the X-1 had been aiming for Mach 1, people down on the ground had been waiting nervously. In the midst of the flight they had been surprised to hear a sound like an explosion or a clap of thunder. It had happened at the moment Chuck had hit Mach 1. That was the first "sonic boom" ever heard on earth.

It was caused by shock waves forming in at least two places on the rocket, the front and the rear. When a supersonic plane is flying at a low enough altitude, the "boom" is not only heard by people on the ground, but it can also be strong enough to crack glass and plaster on a wall!

After reaching Mach 1, Chuck glided down powerless at 300–400 miles per hour. On the way, he performed some aerobatics for the fun of it, rolling about in the sky and doing several wing-overs. At one point when he looked out the window he saw a heavily timbered mountain. It occurred to him that it looked like a good area for hunting, and the man who would forever love the great outdoors wondered if there were a hidden lake nearby where the fishing would be good.

The Bell X-1 rocket shown with a pattern of "shock" diamonds in its wake

USAF

A moment afterward he smoothly glided back onto the field. From the time the X-1 was dropped until that moment of landing, a total of fourteen minutes had passed. After all the time and practice and all the tension built up, it seemed a strangely short amount of time for the climax event!

Although Chuck didn't know exactly what had happened to the Machmeter needle, it was later determined that it had hit 1.04—a bit over and faster than Mach 1!

Cold and fatigued, but highly exhilarated, Chuck turned off the switches and slipped out of his harness, helmet and mask. Then he climbed out of the rocket and was greeted by the groundmen. A briefing was scheduled for the team to review the flight, but Chuck was too tired and asked that the discussion be postponed. For now he just wanted to see Glennis and go home to rest.

He knew what kind of an ordeal she had been through, waiting as she did once again. She, like so many test pilot wives, never knew from day to day if her husband would come home again. But Glennis, no matter how frightened she was, always tried to be supportive of her husband.

How could Chuck, who came to be called "the fastest man in the world," ever describe such an extraordinary experience? Government restrictions prevented Chuck from shouting with joy and relief at the top of his lungs. Instead, his words "It's gone screwy," referring to the Machmeter, seemed to serve as a private code that the crew and other officials understood. A top-secret lid was tightly clamped on this historic event, and unfortunately it remained that way for some time. It was understood that the restrictions were for security reasons so that the United States could keep a competitive edge over Russia in the field of supersonic work.

There was to be neither a big nation-wide announcement nor a celebration, although there was an announcement on the base at Muroc, and a secret ceremony was held a week later in Washington, where Chuck was awarded another Distinguished Flying Cross. Chuck, always the "regular guy," who flew because he liked it and not for rewards, enjoyed a free steak dinner that historical night, served to him courtesy of the one and only restaurant near the base. The owner had promised the dinner to the first pilot who broke the record and lived to tell about it.

Excitement at fever pitch doesn't last forever, though. In *Across the High Frontier,* Chuck's story written by William Lundgren, Chuck described the way he felt the next morning. "There was only a sense of accomplishment, of a deep awareness of the thing I'd done as I went back to work again . . . I was still in the Air Force, still a working pilot assigned to Fighter Test."

A few months later, news of the flight leaked out, but it was not until the following spring that the Air Force, now no longer the Air Corps of the U.S. Army but a separate branch of the military, finally confirmed it. It was important and momentous news. Of course, it didn't have the same impact and excitement there would have been if the news had been broadcast on the day of the event. Nevertheless, with the confirmation of the news, it was just as Chuck had suspected. His private life was never to be the same again. Wherever he went he was applauded.

President Harry Truman presents the Collier Trophy jointly to Capt. Yeager; John Stack, a research scientist (not pictured); and Lawrence Bell.

USAF/NATIONAL AIR AND SPACE MUSEUM, SMITHSONIAN INSTITUTION

He was called to Washington to receive from Chief of Staff General Hoyt Vandenberg the Mackay Trophy for outstanding military aviation performance. Next he was off to the White House for a presentation by President Harry S. Truman. This time it was America's highest aeronautical honor, the thirty-seven-year-old Collier Trophy, awarded by the National Aeronautical Association for "greatest achievement in aviation in America, the value of which had been demonstrated by actual use during the preceding year." This award he shared with two other men, Lawrence Bell, president of the Bell Aircraft Corporation, and John Stack, a government research scientist of the National Advisory Committee for Aeronautics, who was a top designer on the project. The award committee praised each man individually and the three together for the flight that was the "greatest since the first successful flight of the original Wright brothers airplane."

Chuck was not always comfortable dressed in a suit and tie and attending banquets in the nation's capital. But he was famous now, and like it or not, there was no way he could avoid public appearances.

It became even more uncomfortable for him when he was called upon to stand and speak before an audience. "I'm only a fighter pilot. I don't do speeches," he responded to a Washington Pentagon colonel when told that he would have to travel throughout the country addressing military and civilian audiences. Again, he felt self-conscious because of his lack of education and the fact that his grammar might not be perfect. He even remembered how much he disliked giving oral book reports, but he was thankful that his English teacher Virginia Smith had made him stand up in front of the class and practice, despite his protest.

The thought of public speaking gave him the jitters, and he joked that going up in a rocket was much easier. Glennis encouraged Chuck to do his duty by reminding him that he wasn't expected to give great speeches, but that people "just want to see a hero." Chuck, who didn't feel like a hero, answered back jokingly, "Where's a hero? Show me."

Finally, after delivering several short talks that didn't involve technical information, which would be difficult for the public to understand, Chuck began to feel less and less stiff. He began to understand that the public enjoyed meeting someone they viewed as a "hero," who was young and a regular guy just like everyone else. And understanding this, he also felt it was important to answer all his mail and sign all the autographs that were requested of him. Many years later when he met astronaut John Glenn, he advised the astronaut not to use a mechanical writing device to sign his autographs, because he sincerely believed that a child deserved to have the real thing.

In the midst of all this there was one occasion that became a special one for Chuck. After so many nights in hotels in strange cities, he was scheduled to return back home to Lincoln County, West Virginia, as a guest of honor. A nearby Huntington newspaper, *The Advertiser*, announced, "The biggest air show ever staged in Huntington and probably in all West Virginia is scheduled today . . . in tribute to an honored guest, Captain Charles Yeager of Hamlin . . . he is to be welcomed by more than a score of planes aloft and by a parade in downtown Huntington featuring at least seven high school bands and a number of veterans and military organizations. Today has been officially designated Captain Charles Yeager Day."

Chuck was the featured speaker at the Civiton Club luncheon held in a local hotel. It was attended not only by club members, Chuck's family, and Hamlin school officials he knew, but by mayors, governors and generals as well.

On the platform Chuck said with a smile, "When I was a boy in Lincoln County, I heard of the important people who are at this luncheon today. I got to see a few of them. But I didn't think I'd ever get to sit down and eat with them."

No matter what the topic of Chuck's talk at his many public appearances, one comment he made was always the same. He never forgot to speak of the pride he felt wearing an Air Force uniform when he made that first supersonic flight.

At the end of his Civiton Club talk about his X-1 experience, he called himself lucky to have been selected for the job.

After the speech, many people in the audience remarked among themselves how much Chuck was the same folksy fellow they had known before, despite the fact that he was now famous throughout the world.

During the next year, Chuck made more than thirty further test flights in the X-1, and supersonic flying became a weekly routine for him. Odd as it sounded, when he added up his flight hours in the rocket, they totaled only a little more than four hours!

Since the Air Force and Bell were still gathering data on aircraft stability, control and speed at measurements even beyond Mach 1, it was only natural that every flight was not going to run smoothly. Once the crew forgot to complete all the steps in releasing the mechanism that dropped the X-1 from the mothership bomb bay, and Chuck ended up hanging suspended. All he could do was dump the rocket fuel and land with the rocket still attached. But he couldn't stay inside the X-1 cockpit during the landing, so he climbed out and made a dangerous scramble back up the ladder into the B-29.

Another time, one of the worst catastrophies that can happen to a pilot occurred. Fire! Chuck was at 38,000 feet when he heard a noise in back. The fire warning light failed to activate, but he noticed smoke. One of the problems with the rocket was that he couldn't see what was happening behind him. Immediately he turned off the engine, dumped the rest of the fuel and landed, before finding out that insulation near the engine compartment had burned.

But the fire trouble did not end there. During several successive flights, the cabin continued to fill with smoke. The engine was overhauled thoroughly, and Chuck always tried to stay cool, but everyone was still plenty worried. At last the problem was solved when one of the Bell company designers came out to Muroc and figured out that the wrong gaskets had been installed during one of the overhaul sessions.

It was around that time that Col. Boyd decided Chuck had had enough of the X-1 for a while. And he wanted to give a few other pilots a crack at it. Some of those pilots asked Chuck how he had made it look so easy.

Chuck Yeager was only twenty-four the year he won fame by breaking the "sound barrier," and he had come close to death more times than he or Glennis cared to count. It seemed as if he had lived enough adventures for a full lifetime already, but he was only just beginning. His life was to be filled with a great many more.

CHAPTER 8

The Only Place to Be

The Bell X-1 had become a very important part of Chuck's life, and he took deep pride in it.

One day he and the other men at the base learned that the U.S. Navy had started flying jet-powered airplanes from a ground take-off. The X-1 was still being airborne by a mothership, but now the Air Force began to consider it for ground take-off too. Even though Chuck had taken time away from it for a while, he and the Air Force wanted to show what else the mighty X-1 could do. They also figured it would be done in the spirit of friendly competition.

It was going to be risky, though. The rocket had not been designed for ground take-off, so there were plenty of questions to ask. Would it be too heavy for a vertical climb? Would that kind of take-off be too stressful on the landing gear? And since a load that's too heavy would make it hard for the craft to go straight up, would they be able to keep the load of fuel light enough?

All of these factors were discussed and investigated, and it was decided that the X-1 could be prepared for a vertical take-off. This meant shooting to break another record, and for that to happen and be officially credited, it was necessary to get approval from the National Aeronautical Association (NAA). After careful consideration, approval was given. Project engineers agreed that if the ground take-off were performed as planned, it would be a truly spectacular sight.

On January 5, 1949, Chuck confidently climbed into the cockpit of the plane he knew so well. He fired all four rocket chambers, "streaked down the runway," raised the nose and leaped into the air. The X-1 shot up with a vertical velocity of about 13,000 feet per minute. In the short period of only one minute and forty seconds, it reached a height of 23,000 feet. Two and a half minutes after take-off, fuel ran out, so Chuck came down from what he called a "fabulous flight."

Chuck Yeager had done it again! He had broken another record. As the engineers had predicted, it was a "truly spectacular sight."

Afterward, the proud pilot made a phone call to the hospital where Glennis lay in the maternity ward anxiously waiting once again to hear the news. Only a short time before, she had given birth to the Yeagers' first daughter, Sharon.

Chuck continued to fly the X-1 for a while longer after that. Then finally the rocket was "retired" to the National Air and Space Museum of the Smithsonian Institution in Washington, D.C. There it was placed near another history-making airplane—the first one, flown by the Wright Brothers. Speaking about the Bell rocket, a museum official stated, "The X-1 marked the end of the first great period of the air age and the beginning of the second. In a few moments the subsonic period became history, and the supersonic period was born." Later, when Chuck visited the museum and saw the X-1 hanging from a high ceiling in full view near the entrance, he called it "still one of the prettiest little airplanes I've ever seen."

For several years, Chuck tested aircraft of all types, sometimes as many as three or four different kinds in one day. A renowned Air Force pilot who knew Chuck well, Lieut. General James "Jimmy" Doolittle, wrote in the introduction of *Across the High Frontier* that a test pilot gives his research airplane a "good part of his life . . . in the air, he must become a part of it. Together, man and machine must yield the new aeronautical knowledge from which advanced operational aircraft and missiles are evolved." Testing demands were made especially tough during those years because of continual new competition among airplane manufacturers.

The new decade of the 1950s brought another important change. The name of the base, Muroc, officially became Edwards Air Force Base, honoring test pilot Captain Glenn Edwards, who along with his crew was killed during an experimental flight. Edwards Air Force Base grew rapidly. The Yeagers still lived in what they called a "ramshackle" house in the desert. And the famous test pilot continued to risk his life every day as he worked for a regular military salary. But for Chuck, Edwards was "the only place on earth to be if you loved to fly."

Chuck didn't spend all his time testing new craft. He had another important job, and even though there was

USAF

Muroc Air Base, in California's Mojave Desert, became Edwards Air Force Base

no glory in it, he took it as seriously as the rest of his work. It was flying chase for other test pilots. That meant flying alongside a man who was testing a plane to give him help when necessary.

A United States Navy test pilot Bill Bridgeman, in a book coauthored with Jacqueline Hazard entitled *The Lonely Sky,* remembered two incidents when Chuck was flying chase for him. Once, Bill was up in a Douglas plane called the Skyrocket when he ran into trouble. There was a fire warning. The Skyrocket began to spiral downward, and when Bill looked out he saw a stream of black smoke.

His aim was to get the airplane down before the fire reached the engine. If the pilot pressed the button to eject the seat out of the craft to save his life, the four-million-dollar airplane would blow up. Not only that, but there would be no way to determine the cause of damage and provide data on the Skyrocket trouble. That, of course, was an important part of the research.

From the chase plane, where Chuck immediately saw the smoke, he began talking calmly to the panicked pilot. "Manipulate your throttle, Bill, and let's see what it does," Chuck said. "That's it . . . ease her back again . . . when you pull back, it tends to diminish the smoke . . . maybe you had better cut the jet engine . . ."

With his controlled, sure voice, Chuck continued to guide Bill down, all the while giving him the confidence he needed to perform under such pressure. When Bridgeman came in for the landing, Chuck said, "You got it made . . . that's a boy. Nice job." After they had both touched down, Bill hurried to Chuck to thank him for helping to save his life.

"My pleasure," Chuck smiled. "Any time at all." And he turned to leave.

On another occasion when Bridgeman was flying he found himself hampered by a bright, blinding sun. It was shining directly in his eyes, making it almost impossible for him to see the instrument panel.

"I was startled as a shadow fell unexpectedly across my face, blocking the glare out of the cockpit," Bill recalled. "Slightly ahead and above me Yeager was dipping his wing in front of the sun, shading my eyes."

Chuck radioed to Bill. "Is that better, son?"

Although Chuck was younger than many of the other pilots who flew for both the military and for private airplane manufacturers, he came to be known as the "old man" of flight testing. He often found himself calling older men "son," and they never seemed to mind.

There was another time when Chuck's ability, calm and intelligent approach saved a life. It's a story that is well-known at Edwards Air Force Base.

Chuck was flying chase for another pilot, and one morning they took off at dawn. When they were up at 20,000 feet, Chuck suddenly noticed something strange. The other pilot was weaving and flying sloppily. Immediately Chuck realized that the man was in trouble.

Chuck contacted him by radio. "Hey, boy, how do you feel?" he asked.

There was no answer.

It seemed to Chuck that there was only one reason for this strange predicament. He figured the cause was hypoxia, lack of oxygen, and he figured it was probably caused by a disconnected oxygen hose.

Chuck called over again. There was still no response.

Chuck was certain it would only be a matter of minutes before the pilot would pass out, and he tried calling once more. Fortunately this time the pilot answered, but with slurred odd-sounding words, the way a person intoxicated with alcohol or drugs might speak.

That was an indication to Chuck that his guess about the problem of hypoxia was correct. The pilot was definitely losing oxygen.

Chuck had to think fast. Instantly he came up with an idea.

He would pretend *he* was the one in trouble. "Hey, I got a problem here," he said to the pilot. "Follow me down."

Again there was only silence at the other end.

This time Chuck, usually calm and cool, shouted to jolt the man. "Look, my devoted young scientist, follow me down!"

His sudden roar accomplished what he intended, and the pilot obeyed. Chuck got him to come down to a lower altitude, and as soon as he lowered the plane to 12,000 feet, where the air contained more oxygen, the pilot began to feel somewhat normal again.

Chuck kept him talking until his voice was no longer slurred. "How do you feel?" Chuck asked.

"I feel better," the pilot answered. "What happened?"

Later, when the cockpit was examined, Chuck's guess about the problem was confirmed. The oxygen tube had pulled loose.

In this job, Chuck was reminded time and time again that death was always a possibility.

CHAPTER

9

Another Dangerous Risk

December 1953 marked an important date in aviation history. It was the 50th anniversary of flight. On December 17, 1903, the Wright Brothers, Wilbur and Orville, made history at Kitty Hawk, North Carolina, with their first controlled power flight. The record shows that the flight lasted a total of twelve seconds and measured a distance of 120 feet. Their speed was recorded at seven miles per hour.

Half a century later, in 1953, the military wanted to celebrate the anniversary of flight. What better way to do it, they thought, than to break a new record by flying at Mach 2—twice the speed of sound!

Bell Aircraft Corporation had now developed a new airplane, the X-1A. It was similar to the X-1, built low to the ground, with the same tail and short wing design, and again with no ejection seat. This time, however, there was a bubble canopy for better visibility from the cockpit, although Chuck admitted to an aviation magazine writer that he wasn't so sure the improvement gave him peace of mind, since he could actually see the wings buffeting and the shock waves on them.

The Bell X-1A had many improved features over the X-1 rocket.

The most important difference was that the X-1A fuselage was extended seven feet, which allowed it to carry more fuel and provide greater sustained power. That meant, of course, that it could fly several minutes longer.

For months, the X-1A had been the pet project of a flier named "Skip" Zeigler. He was not a military pilot, but a civilian pilot who flew for the Bell Company. In an unfortunate experimental flight incident, however, he was killed, leaving the new aircraft with no one who knew it as intimately as he did. When that happened, officials at Bell asked the Air Force to take over, and once again Chuck Yeager was requested for the job.

He didn't agree to it quite so quickly this time, though. Glennis was expecting their fourth child, a daughter named Susan, and was having a particularly difficult pregnancy. It didn't seem right for Chuck to get involved in such a risky project just then. But after a good deal of thought and discussion and a reasonable amount of reassurance, he finally said yes.

So the former X-1 crew was brought together again—Ridley, Frost and crew chief Jack Russell. It was just like the good old times back in the "early" supersonic days.

Chuck found the X-1A a better airplane, but that didn't mean he could relax and take it for granted. He made sure he learned its every nut and bolt and its control forces, especially its new control stick, which took some extra muscle because winds at high speeds made it pretty stiff and difficult to move. His life depended on knowing this plane just as well as he had come to know the X-1.

The first time Chuck went to take the X-1A up for practice, everything was ready both inside and out. Outside, the fire trucks stood by, along with the crewmen, the sound truck to record on tape all that would happen and the base photographer to set up the motion picture camera. Inside, Chuck went up with the help of a B-50, and this time he didn't have to do any acrobatic climbs on a ladder out in the cold because the B-50 had an "open cockpit" through which he could step down and lower himself directly into the rocket. Following that, Jack Ridley lowered the canopy and bolted it back in place.

Chuck was dropped at 25,000 feet, and the extra 4,000 pounds of fuel the X-1A carried burnt four minutes longer than the fuel in the X-1's. The pilot said the first flight, which took him a little beyond Mach 1, went "beautifully."

So did the second flight, which Chuck described in *Plane Talk*. "I took it up to 50,000 feet, let it sit 'til it got up to 1.5, shut it off and jettisoned the remainder of the liquid oxygen and fuel, and came down and landed. We looked at our data, and I pretty well had the flight plan down perfect, which is important!"

On the third flight he went up to 1.9.

Only days later Mach 2 was hit by a pilot from the National Advisory Committee for Aeronautics, Scott Crossfield.

It came time for Chuck's fourth and final flight. It didn't matter that somebody else had hit Mach 2 first. Chuck was still eager to achieve that speed with the X-1A. The flight took place on December 12, a few days earlier than scheduled. And it was the flight that came closest to being Chuck's last. "That was probably the most trouble I've ever been in," he recalled.

As usual, it was launched from the B-50, released from its bomb bay at 30,000 feet. "One minute to release," the crew chief said.

"Okay, it's hot in here," Chuck responded.

Then, after the one-minute countdown, there came the release, faster and heavier than that of the X-1, but with the familiar cracking sound. The new domed canopy, though, gave Chuck an astonishing view of the shock waves.

"At 45,000 feet we had all four chambers going," he later wrote, "and I shot the X-1A to 72,000 feet and pushed a burst of speed, passing Mach 2." Suddenly, the Machmeter showed that Chuck approached the astounding number of 2.5, two-and-a-half times the speed of sound! (At that altitude, it was recorded at

1,650 miles per hour.) He had gone beyond the maximum speed at which the X-1A was controllable.

But he had gone too high too fast, and he felt himself going "haywire," rolling, falling, experiencing violent, terrifying battering. He lost control, and the plane started spinning earthward with a powerful force. A momentous spin continued until it was making two full rolls per second. The pull was ten positive and four negative *g*'s, which meant he was thrown upward with four times the pull of gravity and forced downward with ten times the pull of gravity.

All of a sudden his pressure suit inflated as it was supposed to do, but as he gasped, his face plate fogged, making it nearly impossible for him to see. "We were spinning down through the sky like a frisbee," he wrote in his autobiography *Yeager*. He tried reaching for the instrument panel for the switch to defog the face plate, "but then the ship snapped violently back on itself, slamming me against the control stick and somehow hooking my helmet onto it. As I struggled to get free I had glimpses of light and dark, light and dark, through the fogged visor. Sun, ground, sun, ground. Spinning down. I had less than a minute left."

Later Chuck explained, "I rolled the stabilizer in, but overshot and the airplane got into an inverted spin, so I came back to neutral, put everything with the inverted spin, flipped into a normal spin, and I recovered at 25,000 feet. I was hurting pretty badly by the time I got the airplane on its back." Somehow after that he managed to glide back and come in for a landing.

He had spun down more than 51,000 feet in fifty-one seconds. That was a distance of about ten miles. He believed that he had "survived on sheer instinct and pure luck."

No test pilot's day is ordinary. But this, December 12, 1953, was the most unusual of his career so far. That evening, following his new, incredible speed record and his terrifying life and death experience, he drove with Glennis seventy miles to Los Angeles to appear at a scheduled Army-Navy Club dinner. There he dined, chatted with old friends, met new people and stood up at the podium and delivered a speech!

This time, news of Chuck's astonishing feat was not kept secret by the government. A United Press newspaper story announced, "Major Charles E. Yeager has flown two and one-half times the speed of sound—about 1,650 miles an hour—in the Air Force's X-1A rocket plane, it was reported today. Informed sources said the West Virginia–born test pilot achieved the record-shattering speed Saturday in a flight over Edwards Air Force Base, California."

More awards and trophies were to come. There was the Harmon International Air Trophy Award, the Distinguished Service Medal in recognition of his contributions to science, the Air Force Flight Trophy and the General Mitchell Memorial Trophy, which he shared with General Curtis LeMay.

At a White House ceremony, receiving the Harmon Trophy, Chuck came face to face again with someone he hadn't seen for many years. They were meeting under completely different circumstances now. It was Dwight D. Eisenhower, the man who had helped "evadee" Chuck return to his fighter squadron during the war when government policy was going to force Chuck to be

DWIGHT D. EISENHOWER LIBRARY

U.S. President Dwight D. Eisenhower presented the Harmon International Trophy to Major Yeager at the White House in 1954. Chuck's friend, aviator Jacqueline Cochran, also received a trophy.

sent home. This time, however, Eisenhower was President of the United States, and he singled out Major Chuck Yeager as "one of aviation's genuine pioneers."

Chuck was not the only recipient of the Harmon Trophy at the White House presentation. Also receiving recognition that day was a friend and former student of his. She was Jacqueline Cochran, a renowned aviator, who had broken several women's speed records, won numerous flight awards and during wartime had established and directed the Women's Air Force Service Pilots, under which more than a thousand women aviators had been trained. (She also created and owned a cosmetics business, and it was told that she often reapplied her make-up after a flight landing, before exiting her plane.) Chuck had taught her jet flying, flown chase for her and guided her to reach Mach 1, making her the first woman to fly faster than the speed of sound. Jackie Cochran and her businessman husband Floyd Odlum had also become close personal friends of Chuck and Glennis, so Chuck felt a special pride as Jackie stood side by side with him that day in Washington, D.C., being recognized by President Eisenhower.

Later, Lawrence Bell further publicly recognized Chuck after his record-breaking X-1A flight: "I think the record will show that this airplane—all the X-1s, I should say—is probably the most valuable research airplane the government has ever had. It's had quite a career, that airplane has. And so have you."

CHAPTER

10

Wide, Wide World

For all the flying he had done over the years, no one could say that luck hadn't been riding alongside Charles E. Yeager in the cockpit. But there came a time when Chuck, his family and his fellow workers seriously worried about his pushing that good fortune too long and too far. So Chuck decided that he ought to put the days of dangerous, rigorous flight testing work behind him.

In 1954, he left Edwards, which by then had grown to a large, active Air Force base employing thousands of people. With the departure Chuck left flight testing for operational flying.

Nearly a decade after the end of World War II, Germany and the United States were now joined in alliance against the threat of war with Russia. Chuck was assigned to Hahn Air Base in West Germany, flying F-86 Sabre jets in a tactical fighter squadron.

Chuck, Glennis and the four children enjoyed living in Europe. After years in the California desert, the children had a wonderful time playing in the winter snows and experiencing their first white Christmas.

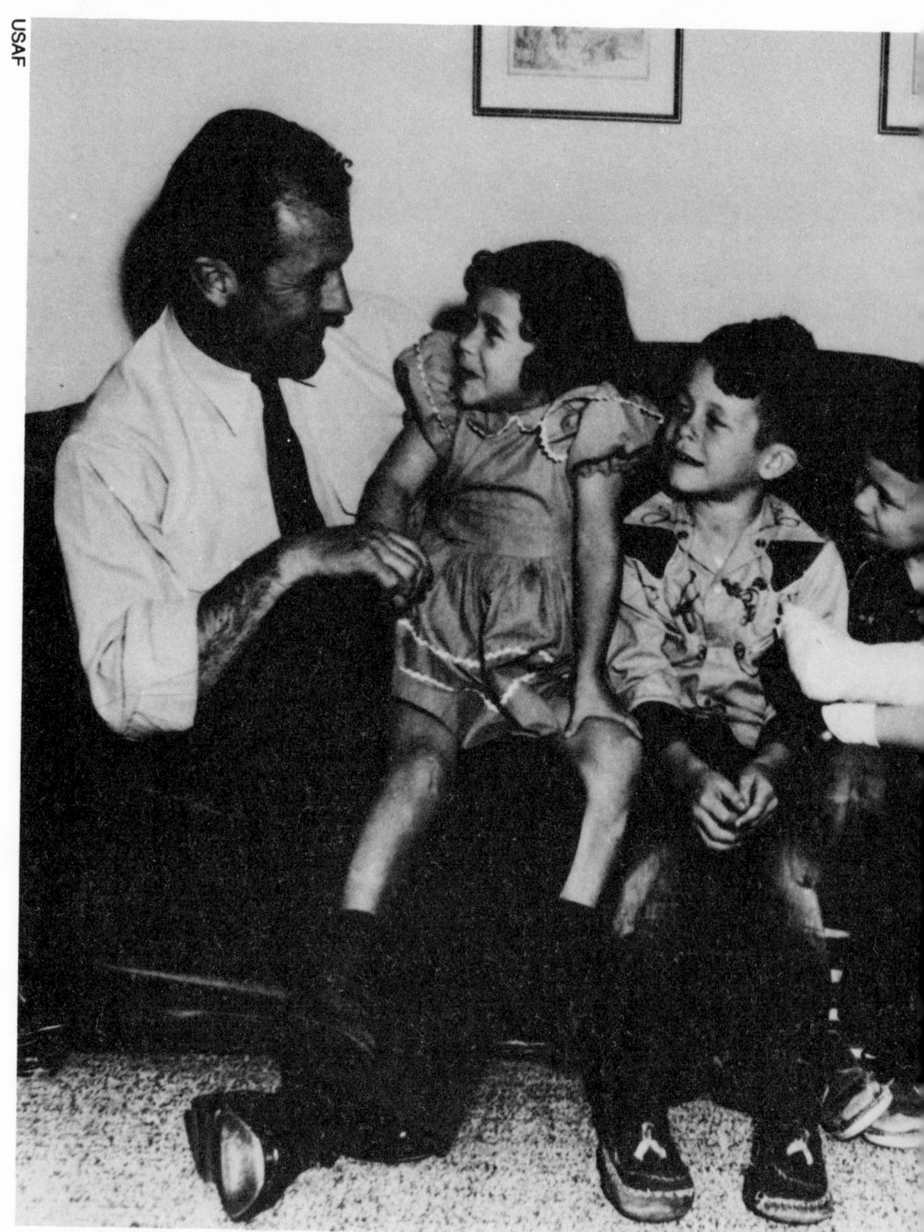

USAF

The Yeager family—Chuck, Sharon, Donald, Michael, Glennis and Susan

On the job, Chuck was glad to be back in the warm camaraderie of a squadron. There with the 417th Fighter Squadron he earned high respect from his men. Colonel Fred Ascani (later to become a Major General), a group commander at Hahn and a man with whom Chuck had worked back in the United States, saw Chuck not only as a remarkable pilot, but as a person extraordinarily "insightful about airplane engineering." Ascani said of Chuck, "There was just no one else like him."

While Chuck was stationed in Germany, the United States was involved in the Korean War. Korea was a divided country. Communist-ruled North Korea, which was supported by Russian troops, had invaded South Korea, and the United States had joined South Korea in its fight to defend its freedom.

In the middle of this war, Chuck was called away from the base at Hahn to take on an unusual job at Okinawa, an island in the western Pacific Ocean which the United States had captured from Japan during World War II. The Air Force had built an air base there.

A North Korean pilot had defected and flown his plane out of his designated region until he landed on Okinawa. He had secretly slipped out of his Communist-controlled country, hoping to take refuge living in a country governed by a democratic system.

The plane the Korean pilot had flown was a Soviet MIG-15, a well-known Russian fighter aircraft that American pilots had flown against in battle. It was supposed to be the fastest, most high-flying and best fighter airplane in combat with America's Sabres over Korea.

Now the United States Air Force had a chance to study this Russian airplane for the first time. Because of his expertise with airplanes, Chuck was immediately called to examine it and try it out for the purpose of gathering data about its climb rate, speed and power.

The weather was bad. There were heavy winds and rains. It was far from an ideal situation for testing a plane like that, but there was no telling how long the storm conditions would last. So Chuck and another test pilot, Tom Collins, decided to go ahead and try it anyway. First Chuck went over the plane, especially making certain that the ejection seat was wired properly. He didn't want to take any chances on not being able to bail out if he hit a major problem. Then with his co-pilot he climbed in and took it up. He was so familiar with airplanes that he was able to fly it, not only in bad weather, but without an instruction manual for the foreign aircraft.

After the flight he concluded that the MIG-15 was "a pretty good fighting machine," but not as sophisticated as American technology. He determined that it had plenty of problems, including pitching its nose up unexpectedly, poor pressurization and a problem going into spins. With so many rough spots like that, he concluded, the pretty good fighting machine was actually a "flying booby trap." These were extremely important conclusions to bring back to the United States Air Force.

There was a lesson to be learned from this experience too, some of the pilots realized. Just because it is the enemy aircraft doesn't mean it should always be held only in complete fear.

It seemed that wherever Chuck went and whatever new airplanes he worked with, he was always considered to possess an extraordinary sixth sense. An Air Force lieutenant, Nate "Rube" Goldberg, called Chuck an "aircraft diagnostician," which meant he had an especially keen ability to diagnose a plane with a problem.

Goldberg remembered an incident on an airfield in Italy. A Sabre jet had broken down and a young pilot stood puzzled over it. When he was approached, he explained that he was waiting for his squadron commander to come and take a look at it.

"Sure enough," said Goldberg, retelling the incident, "a while later I saw Chuck Yeager out there on the airfield with that jet. He looked it over for no more than a few minutes, listened to the engine, went over to the mechanics nearby and told them exactly what was wrong. Forty-five minutes later that puzzled young pilot was on his way."

After three years in Europe, Chuck, who was now promoted to the rank of lieutenant colonel, returned to the United States with the challenging new job of commander to a squadron flying F-100 Super Sabres. The F-100 was an airplane he had test-flown earlier at Edwards.

The Yeagers found themselves back in the desert again, this time fifty miles from Edwards at George Air Force Base. It was not easy for Glennis to return to dusty winds and sand and isolation, but Chuck was eager for this assignment. The arrangement they made to ease the problem of daily living discomfort was to buy a house in nearby Victorville. There at least they had some trees and a little shade, and the town afforded good schooling for the children, which was an important concern to the family.

At that time the world of aircraft was changing rapidly.

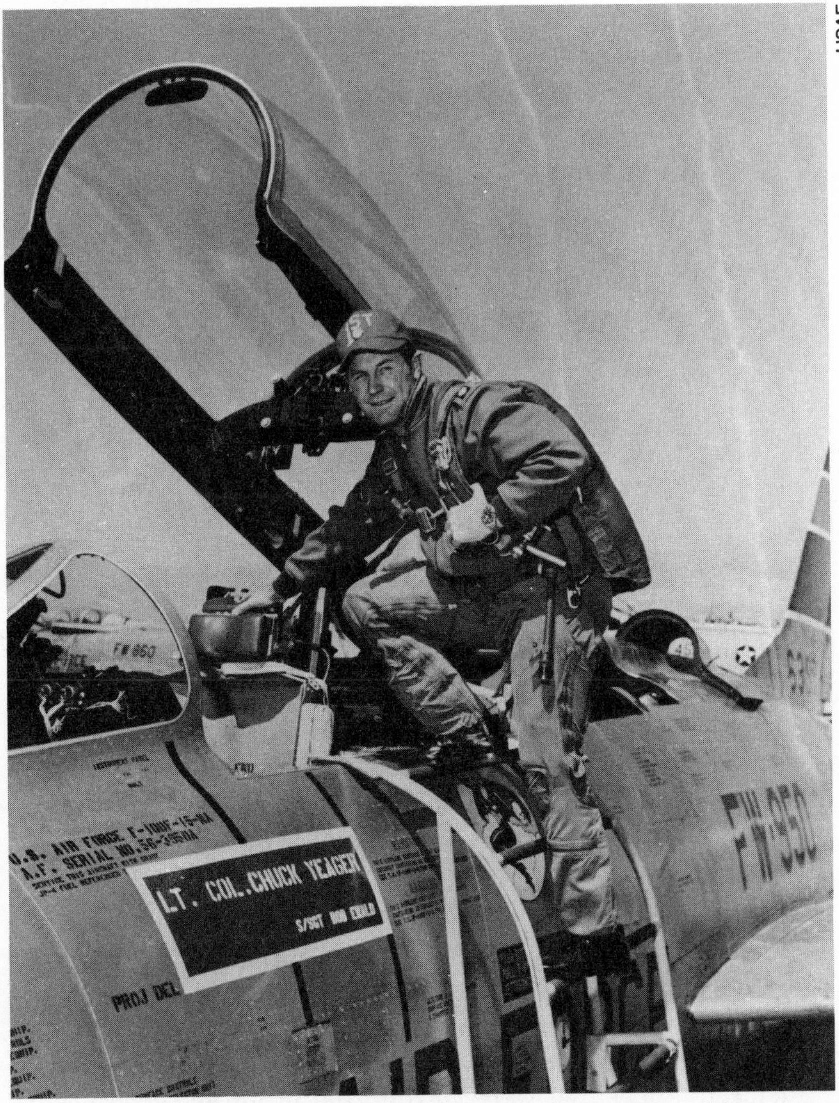

USAF

Lt. Col. Yeager at George Air Force Base, as Commander, First Daylight Air Defense Squadron

There were constantly new developments on all levels, and Chuck was glad to be involved in some of these new operations and in sophisticated novel weaponry techniques.

Just a short time ago, for example, there had been no way for planes to refuel while in flight without landing. But now airborne refueling, which was highly important in military aviation, was being developed. Large bomber aircraft were converted to tankers carrying fuel for transfer to fighters. It required the tanker and the fighter plane to fly together in formation, an especially difficult task for the fighter plane, which had to slow down to 200 miles per hour. Furthermore, it meant maneuvering the fighter into a position to insert a probe into a funnel at the end of a long hose extended by the tanker. It was a bit like stopping off at a "gas station in the sky." It was difficult enough to learn aerial refueling under normal conditions, but in bad weather, it posed an extraordinarily tense and tough challenge.

This system was one that Chuck required his squad to practice over and over under all kinds of conditions until the men were proficient and confident. Like their commander, his men took deep pride not only in their proficiency, but in their good safety record as well. Chuck believed in excellent maintenance of all their planes, which contributed to the group's commendable safety record at the base.

It was during this time at George that Chuck decided to shoot for another record. This attempt, however, had consequences that were far different from the success of his other two.

A new airplane had been developed. It was Lockheed's Starfighter NF-104, which had a rocket engine mounted over the tailpipe. The hydrogen peroxide and fuel would give 6,000 pounds of engine thrust. The craft was to go up as high as 120,000–140,000 feet.

Chuck had flight-tested it a few years earlier, and he had taken a liking to the rocket. It really moved! But before the students at the Aerospace Research Pilot School (ARPS) began flying it, he wanted to check it out. It had not been taken above 100,000 feet yet. No one was sure exactly how it would react up in that thin air. The most important area Chuck hoped to test on those runs was that of the altitude limits. He wanted to determine at what altitude the aerodynamic pitch-up forces would exceed the amount of rocket thrust. The pitch-up problem with the plane's nose was likely to happen when the rocket was flown at a certain angle, causing the nose to rise too suddenly.

Chuck also decided that while he was checking it out, he would try to beat a recent record that was set by the Soviet Union with one of their new jets. Besides, it had been a long time since he had broken a speed record back when he hit Mach 2.5 in the X-1A.

Three times he took the NF-104 up, pushing it higher with each flight. Everything was going well, so at that point he felt ready to give it his all.

With his friend Bud Anderson flying chase, Chuck took off. As soon as he reached an altitude of 40,000 feet, he began his speed run. Then as he neared 100,000 feet he swooped over in an arc, topping out at 104,000 feet. This was twenty miles up in space!

But as he came back down from that arc he had formed, he met real trouble. Unexpectedly, the nose

Chuck taking off in the NF-104 Starfighter. This flight ended in tragedy and near death when the airplane went into a spin and he had to bail out.

UPWARD
EJECTION
SEAT
CANOPY RELEASE
RESCU
EMERGENCY ENT
CONTROL ON OT
SIDE
ORCE

USAF

pitched up. Alarmed, Chuck pushed the control to bring the nose down, but nothing happened. He hit the thruster and the reaction controls, but still nothing happened.

Then he started dropping. All of a sudden, at 100,000 feet, the plane went into a flat spin. He realized that the hydrogen peroxide was gone, yet there was a fair amount of fuel left in the main engine. But what did that really matter? There was no way to relight it now anyway. Meanwhile he just kept spinning and whirling. He felt as if he were being ripped apart.

All the time he kept his eyes fixed on the instrument panel. If he didn't keep them fixed on something, he would suffer from vertigo, severe dizziness and illness, and he would never be able to regain control. Even so, he knew there was not one emergency action he could take. That left only one thing to do. Eject the seat and bail out!

With barely minutes to lose, he reached under the seat and pulled the cinch ring. Whack! Out of the cockpit he and his seat were thrust upward a force of 90 miles per hour. It happened with such powerful impact that for a moment he felt as if he'd been knocked unconscious. He could hardly see. He could hardly think, but he was aware of the parachute popping open. Then slowly he began to come to his senses, and when he did, he saw the ejected seat floating right above him. Underneath it, Chuck saw the gaping hole in the airplane where the ejecting mechanism had been attached to it, and inside that hole were the remains of the rocket propellant. To his horror, it glowed bright, hot red.

Then all of a sudden the parachute lines became

tangled with the floating seat. Chuck continued to fall, but it seemed more like he was falling in a terrifying nightmare. To make the nightmare even worse, a second later he was yanked up by the parachute lines and smashed in the face by the 80-pound metal seat. It had cracked right through the helmet visor, completely shutting his left eye.

The seat fell away, but Chuck was left stunned. Not only that, he was on fire! A flash fire inside his helmet!

The rocket propellant from the seat had set flames to the rubber seal between the helmet and pressure suit. Flames and smoke engulfed his head. There he was, still tumbling through the air, choking and suffocating with smoke. During this ordeal he managed to reach his hand inside the face plate to allow for some air to breathe and to shut off the oxygen that kept feeding the flames. But his gloved hand caught fire too.

When he hit the ground he came down hard. He was dazed and in intense pain. Miraculously he pulled himself to his feet and staggered to the road, where a few minutes later he was rescued.

Chuck remained in the hospital for a little more than a month while the flight surgeon, Dr. Stanley Bear, kept careful watch over him, regularly scraping the patient's charred skin in a painful procedure to prevent scarring. Chuck's sight in his damaged eye, the doctor explained, had been saved by a heavy crust of blood that had formed over the eye.

Chuck had not been able to break a record in the NF-104. And he never tried to push his luck like that again.

In his book *Yeager*, he wrote that thoughts of death were often in his mind while he was in combat and during his years of flight testing. "Death is the great enemy and robber in my profession, taking away so many friends over the years, all of them young," he wrote. And "facing death takes many kinds of courage." But test pilots don't fly for glory or money. They enjoy flying. They are also dedicated and fly because they feel a strong sense of duty and loyalty to their country. For this, Charles Yeager of the United States Air Force was always proud.

After that, Chuck went to the Air War College at Maxwell Air Force Base in Alabama, the Air Force's senior professional military education school that prepared selected colonels and lieutenant colonels for key leadership and responsibility positions. There in the resident program Chuck attended lectures and seminars and participated in exercises involving areas such as aerospace power and national security policy.

When he graduated from the Air War College he also earned the rank of full colonel, and one year later he was appointed Commandant of the Aerospace Research Pilot School (ARPS) at Edwards. This was the training ground for the future pioneers who explored space.

Then in 1966 he took command of the 405th Fighter Wing at Clark Air Base in the Philippines. There he was assigned charge of five squadrons throughout Southeast Asia during the Vietnam War. Like Korea, Vietnam was a country torn in two, with North Vietnam having come under Communist domination. For years the North had infiltrated the South until the South began to lose its hold. Concerned about stopping further Communist dominance there and also throughout the world, the United States sent troops into Vietnam to help the

South. But there were many Americans who felt the United States shouldn't be involved there at all. It was a confusing war that Chuck and his comrades were fighting in, but they were military men, and once again they were doing their military job.

They were in combat now, using sophisticated new weaponry guided by radar and lasers and the most up-to-date communications systems, but the Communist weaponry developed in Russia was always a match. Besides the constant danger and tragic events involved in fighting a war, Chuck was faced with the enormous and difficult job of commanding a fighter wing, which meant overseeing five squadron commanders and the men under them who were spread out over thousands of miles. Because of that, he often wrestled with the feeling that too much was out of his control. He worked hard at trying to lessen that problem, and one method that helped was to call regular review sessions with his top men to keep contact as close as possible. In the middle of this turmoil, Chuck also managed to fly 128 combat missions himself.

Not all travel took Chuck into areas of flight work or combat across the globe. A European trip that he and Glennis took for pleasure turned out to be a particularly heartwarming one. They journeyed back to the province in France where Chuck's life had been saved, a place that he remembered with deep affection. The town of Nérac still stood. And M. Gabriel, the brave Frenchman who had taken such good care of him, was easy to find. He was the mayor!

Chuck also revisited Madame Starodvorsky, the woman who had questioned him in English to make sure he was not an enemy spy. At the time of the reunion, Madame Starodvorsky was 84 years old, but she remembered every detail of Chuck's rescue and the conversation she had had with him. She even remembered that he came from a state in America called West Virginia.

During their stay in Nérac, a gala banquet was held in honor of the two American visitors, and a toast was proposed to the "brave Monsieur Yeager and the charming Madame Yeager."

Afterward Chuck told a reporter from the military newspaper *Stars and Stripes* that it had been a "real pleasure for the opportunity of reliving the past with those who laid their necks on the line for me."

When Chuck was back in the United States, this time stationed at the base of Seymour Johnson in North Carolina, he received an unexpected telephone call one day. It was from a vice commander at U.S. Air Force Tactical Air Command, the mobile strike force that deploys, or sends out, combat-ready air forces anywhere in the world for national security. The caller's message took Chuck by surprise. Chuck was informed that he was being promoted to brigadier general. This was a highly distinguished honor that he had won over hundreds of other nominees, whose records were evaluated by the selection board, the Secretary of the Air Force and the President of the United States.

Chuck later remembered being "stunned" at the news. He had never thought that someone like him, a high school graduate who had begun training under the "flying sergeant program," could ever be honored with such recognition.

It had been a long time since a young boy in Hamlin

USAF

Brigadier General Chuck Yeager in an F-15 at Edwards Air Force Base

had told a family friend he might just become an army general someday. Now that "someday" had actually arrived, and this time instead of the Smiths, Chuck was doing the smiling. Charles E. Yeager had become a brigadier general of the United States Air Force, and he wore his new star on his uniform with his head held high.

By this time the exciting new Space Age had arrived. As commander of ARPS at Edwards, he had helped select and train astronauts in precision flying necessary for orbiting space labs and shuttles and sustaining weightlessness for extended periods.

Chuck, who had so much knowledge about altitude flying, had hoped to be able to experience weightless flying himself, but the project passed into the hands of new and younger men. Besides, it seemed that since his days at Muroc, Brigadier General Chuck Yeager had already lived many lives. He had raised a family of four children with his wife Glennis, been all over the globe, flown 180 different kinds of military aircraft, logged some 10,000 flying hours, escaped death numerous times, made aviation history with his record-breaking feats, and gained world-wide acclaim. Maybe there came a time for a man, even someone like Chuck Yeager, to consider retirement.

11

Reach for the Heights

Chuck was working next to Edwards at Norton Air Base as safety director of the Air Force when his retirement ceremony was held there in 1975. Friends, former crew and military men from the top ranks on down flew out to Norton to honor Brigadier General Chuck Yeager that day. Emotions ran deep, honoring a man and his remarkable career.

For some time to come, Chuck continued receiving awards, including a special peacetime Congressional Medal of Honor presented to him by President Gerald Ford, which brought Chuck to the White House once again. He was also enshrined in the Aviation Hall of Fame in Dayton, Ohio, with the presentation made by his friend Jackie Cochran, and he was further paid homage at Edwards by the unveiling of a large oil painting of himself and the Bell X-1, which was hung in the base officer's club lobby.

Once he was officially retired, Chuck moved with Glennis into a redwood house in the Sierra foothills near Grass Valley, California. It was beautiful country that afforded Chuck the immediate pleasures of hiking, hunting and fishing, especially going after golden trout. In an interview with *People* magazine he said, "Years ago when I was flying over the Mount Whitmore area, I spotted a lake way up in the High Sierra—clear and teeming with trout, up there above the timberline—Crabtree Lake it's called, at 13,000 feet, and the golden trout spawn in there. We pack in on foot 125 miles away . . . finding that lake, just with the luck of the flight pattern—that's one of the real rewards of flying."

He and Glennis spent a good deal of time visiting their children and grandchildren, and they even "adopted a baby" of their own to care for—a pet quail, whose mother had been killed by a hawk. Chuck might have remembered with special fondness the book he had read and reported on in Miss Smith's English class—*Crooked Bill, the Life of a Quail*.

For a while it seemed that retirement for a man of such action and adventure was too quiet for Chuck, and hiking and fishing weren't quite enough to satisfy him. So he took up hang-gliding and carpentry and began to split his own wood, which he said "makes exercise a pleasure." He was also glad for a new kind of part-time job when he was hired by Northrop Corporation, an aircraft manufacturer, as a consulting test pilot, giving him a chance to fly the new F-20 Tigershark, a Mach-2 aircraft.

Chuck entered show business too. He was portrayed by actor Sam Shepard in a 1983 movie called *The Right Stuff*, filmed from the book of the same title written by Tom Wolfe, and served as a technical consultant to the film crew. He played a small part in the movie as well, that of a "tough guy" in a saloon near Muroc where pilots gathered. He also played himself as an Air Force officer in one episode of a television series, "I Dream of Jeannie," and made a TV commercial for a company that manufactures automobile parts.

One day Chuck became the star of a television show without knowing it was going to happen. It began with what he believed to be an arrangement for a *Right Stuff* movie publicity interview he was told would be scheduled in Los Angeles. He was picked up at the Los Angeles airport, driven to the NBC studio, and led into a dressing room.

There an actor joined him, only instead of beginning a publicity interview, he began talking into a microphone about "spinning back to a great name in history." Chuck still didn't suspect anything out of the ordinary, but when the actor told him, "We have a little surprise for you," and Chuck saw a hidden camera, then an audience and finally the TV host, Ralph Edwards, he realized exactly what was going on. At that moment Ralph Edwards stepped forward, led Chuck to the center of a stage and announced, "Tonight, Charles E. Yeager, this is your life!"

Chuck had been "tricked" and surprised at being chosen the subject for the show, "This is Your Life," which weekly featured a different famed person, presenting the story of his or her life and bringing out surprise guests from that person's past and present life. It was always a bit of a shock when the subjects suddenly found themselves on camera.

Ralph Edwards talked about Chuck's childhood back in Hamlin, and Chuck's brother Hal Jr. and math teacher

Working as a consultant for Northrop Corporation, assisting in the design and development of the Tigershark

NORTHROP CORPORATION

Mrs. Ossie Smith made guest entrances first. Then there was Glennis, who related how she and Chuck had met and married, and she was followed by old friends, Dick Frost and Bud Anderson, who both talked about their experiences flying with Chuck. Finally, the Yeager children, Donald, Michael, Sharon and Susan, and Chuck's grandchildren, joined him, ending the show with an exciting family reunion.

Several years later, in the early 1980s, Chuck became involved in an altogether new project that dealt with something that had always held importance for him—an institution of higher learning. From his leadership in that project, there came into existence a program called The Marshall University Society of Yeager Scholars. Since Chuck believed strongly in dedication to excellence and an inner drive for success to "be the best," it was his intention to arrange to offer dedicated and caring high school students an opportunity for an excellent college education at Marshall University in Huntington, West Virginia. That was just a short distance from his own home town of Hamlin.

Under the direction of Chuck Yeager as Honorary Chairman of the Board of Directors, along with some thirty board members, the program took two years of planning. It was designed to invite high school seniors across the nation to apply for the scholarship, while twenty would be selected each year to receive four years of special education and enrichment at the university with no cost to the student. The scholarship continues through private fundraising.

The Society of Yeager Scholars program was launched in December 1985 at the Smithsonian Air and Space

MARSHALL UNIVERSITY

A medallion was designed for the Society of Yeager Scholars program at Marshall University

MARSHALL UNIVERSITY

Brigadier General Charles E. Yeager speaking at Marshall University Commencement to the graduating class of 1985. (Photo by Rick Haye)

Museum in Washington, D.C. In a speech there, Chuck discussed how once the only "barrier" in the sky turned out to be just a myth, but nearly four decades later he believed another barrier existed—one in the world of higher education that sometimes limited young people from achieving greater intellectual and social development. He explained that with the program he hoped to help "break that barrier" for many of the nation's young people.

"I've joined with Marshall because some very intelligent, very creative people there have designed a thoroughly unconventional academic program that I think will greatly increase the odds of young people achieving excellence in whatever they decide to do with their lives," he said. The program, he continued, has been designed to guide the scholars to "become our leaders of tomorrow by challenging them again and again in every way to rise above the norm, to be better than they can possibly imagine."

A great deal of excitement was generated, and Chuck, the board of directors and the university were eager with anticipation for the fall of 1987. That was the date the first selected group of scholars entered Marshall University, all because of Chuck Yeager's dedication and caring.

Those qualities that Chuck hopes will be nurtured in more and more young people are the very qualities that he himself possessed and that enabled him to reach the heights he did. Chuck, whom his friend Dick Frost called "the best pilot this country has produced," is quick to explain that while some say he had a natural feel for aviation, still "it was hard work, really a lifetime's experience."

Glossary

AEROBATICS—Skilled maneuvers involving spins, loops and rolls performed by the pilot in the aircraft.

ALTITUDE—Height in feet or meters above sea level, which is measured precisely in determining the performance of an aircraft.

BOMB BAY—An area underneath a bomber's fuselage equipped with doors through which a bomb can be dropped.

CENTRIFUGE—A fast rotating machine used to test the ability to withstand gravitational forces.

DRAG—The resistance of air to an object moving through it. The faster an object moves, the more drag it creates. An airplane creates a great amount of drag (drag force is measured in pounds). The more streamlined an airplane is designed, the less drag it produces. The less drag an airplane produces, the faster it can fly.

FLIGHT CONTROLS—The three main flight controls that maintain or change the altitude of an airplane are the *rudder* (a vertical control surface on the tail that causes yawing, or sideways motion), the *ailerons* (dual-hinged, moveable surfaces near wing tips that cause side to side rolling motion) and the *elevator* (a horizontal, moveable control surface at the rear pushing the tail either up or down and causing the airplane nose to rise or lower in the opposite direction).

FUSELAGE—The airplane's body, or main structure, to which are attached the wings, tail, etc.

GASKET—Material, like rubber or metal, to seal an enclosed area under pressure to keep a substance such as steam or gas from leaking.

GLIDE—A controlled descent toward a landing in non-powered flight.

GRAVITY—A natural force that makes objects move or tend to move toward the center of the earth. The earth pulls any object toward it, and so do the moon, planets and stars. Isaac Newton's law of gravitational action states that there is a force of attraction between any two massive particles in the universe.

HYPOXIA—A physiological problem that occurs in pilots when they suffer decreased oxygen in the body tissues because they have less oxygen in the air to breathe. This happens mostly at altitudes above 10,000 feet. Some early symptoms are loss of sense of reality and judgment, loss of ability to think clearly, sluggishness or drowsiness and reduced vision.

JET POWER—One of Newton's laws of motion explains this: for every action, there is an equal and opposite reaction. A jet engine's exhaust is the action, and the thrust is the reaction. To experience action = reaction, blow up a balloon and let it go. The air escapes in one direction (the action), while the balloon moves in another (the reaction).

LIFT—The force supporting the weight of an airplane. This force of lift must be equal to the weight of the airplane in order for the airplane to make a constant climb and maintain a constant glide and level flight. If the lift is more than the weight, the airplane accelerates upward. If the lift is less than the weight, the airplane accelerates downward.

MACH—The Mach number indicates jet airspeed in terms of the speed of sound, which is determined at 761 miles per hour at sea level (less above 45,000 feet as sound doesn't travel as fast in cold air). Mach 1 is an air speed equal to the speed of sound. Mach 2 is equal to twice that. Speeds less than Mach 1 are called *subsonic*. Speeds greater than Mach 1 are called *supersonic* and create Mach or shock waves.

MACHMETER—An instrument used for Mach readings, which automatically compensates, or adjusts, for altitudes and temperature differences.

SHOCK WAVES—Abrupt air pressure disturbances that build up and lock tightly together when an aircraft is traveling at supersonic speeds, forming what might be called powerful speeding shells of compressed air.

SONIC BOOM—A "boom" sound heard on the ground, caused by shock waves either attaching to the airplane nose and tail or traveling on after the passage of the aircraft.

TAKE-OFF—A flight's beginning, which requires lift from the wings to overcome the weight of the airplane. Take-off is best when flying directly into the wind (upwind) so the air flows over the wings.

THRUST—The force created by engine power to overcome drag. For an airplane to maintain constant air speed, the thrust and the drag must be equal. If thrust is greater than drag, the airplane speeds up; if thrust is less than drag, the airplane slows down.

WING-OVER—An airplane maneuver involving making a steep climb, dropping the nose sharply, making a half roll and returning to normal flight in the opposite direction.

INFORMATION SOURCES

United States Air Force, Edwards Air Force Base
Northrop Corporation
National Air and Space Museum, Smithsonian Institution
Marshall University, Huntington, West Virginia

BIBLIOGRAPHY

Berger, Michael. *An Album of Modern Aircraft Testing*. New York: Franklin Watts, 1981.

Bridgeman, Bill, and Jacqueline Hazard. *The Lonely Sky*. New York: Holt, Rinehart and Winston, 1955.

"Chuck Yeager, An American Original." *Modern Maturity*, Oct.–Nov. 1983.

Cross, Roy. *Great Aircraft and Their Pilots*. Greenwich, CT: New York Graphic Society, Ltd., 1972.

Current Biography, 1954. "Charles E. Yeager."

"Fastest Man and the Men Not Far Behind." *Newsweek*, Feb. 22, 1954.

Jones, Robert F. "Chuck Yeager, the Man with the Real Right Stuff, Never Even Got into Space." *People* Magazine, Nov. 21, 1983.

Kuempffert, Waldemar. "Into the Mystery Zone of Supersonic Speed." *The New York Times* Magazine, June 20, 1948.

Lundgren, William. *Across the High Frontier, the Story of a Test Pilot*. New York: William Morrow, 1955.

"Man in a Hurry." *Time* Magazine, April 18, 1949.

Neely, F. R. "Trophy for Flight Beyond the Speed of Sound." *Colliers* Magazine, Dec. 25, 1948.

Price, Wesley. "They Flew Our X-Ships." *Saturday Evening Post*, July 1, 1950.

Sullivan, George. *They Flew Alone*. New York: Warne.

Thomas, Shirley. *Men In Space*. Philadelphia: Chilton Company, 1960.

Wolfe, Tom. *The Right Stuff*. New York: Farrar, Straus, Giroux, 1979.

Yeager, Charles E. "On Flying Faster than Mach 1 and Mach 2." In: *Plane Talk*, Carl R. Oliver, ed. Boston: Houghton Mifflin, 1950.

Yeager, Charles, as told to Adie Suehsdorf. "I Flew Faster than Sound." *This Week* Magazine, April 22, 1949.

Yeager, Chuck, and Leo Janos. *Yeager*. New York: Bantam, 1985.

PERSONAL INTERVIEWS AND CORRESPONDENCE

Hettie Rousch, librarian, Hamlin Public Library
Hal Yeager, Jr., brother
Jake Marcum, former Hamlin residence
Virginia Smith, teacher
Homer Hager, Jr., friend
Paul Bowles, in Chuck's fighter squadron
Charles Kreiner, Bell Aerospace Textron, Buffalo, NY
Colonel Nate "Rube" Goldberg, U.S.A.F. (Ret.)

Index

INDEX

DATE			